A WOMAN AND HER GOD

a WOMAN
AND
HER GOD

LIFE-ENRICHING MESSAGES *featuring*

BETH MOORE,

JILL BRISCOE, SANDRA D. WILSON,
KATHLEEN HART, DAVID HAGER,
THELMA WELLS *and* BEVERLY LAHAYE

INTEGRITY®
PUBLISHERS
Nashville

AMERICAN ASSOCIATION OF
AACC
CHRISTIAN COUNSELORS

A Woman and Her God

Published by Integrity Publishers, a division of Integrity Media, Inc., 5250 Virginia Way, Suite 110, Brentwood, TN 37027 in association with American Association of Christian Counselors.

HELPING PEOPLE WORLDWIDE EXPERIENCE *the* MANIFEST PRESENCE *of* GOD.

Published in association with Yates and Yates, LLP, Literary Agents, Orange, California.

Unless otherwise indicated, Scripture quotations are taken from the Holy Bible, New International Version (NIV). Copyright © 1973, 1978, 1984 International Bible Society. Used by permission of Zondervan Bible Publishers.

Other Scripture quotations are from the following sources:

The Holy Bible, New Living Translation (NLT), copyright © 1996. Used by permission of Tyndale House Publishers, Inc., Wheaton, Illinois. All rights reserved. The New King James Version (NKJV), © 1979, 1980, 1982, Thomas Nelson, Inc., Publishers.

Cover Design: Brand Navigation (www.brandnavigation.com)
Cover Photo: Veer

Library of Congress Cataloging-in-Publication Data
A woman and her God / by Beth Moore . . . [et al].
  p. cm.
"The American Association of Christian Counselors and The Center for Biblical Counseling."
ISBN 1-59145-055-1 (hardcover)
ISBN 1-59145-204-X (paperback)
1. Christian women—Religious life. I. Moore, Beth. II. American Association of Christian Counselors. III. Center for Biblical Counseling (U.S.)
BV4527.W587   2003
248.8'43–dc21   2003040737

Printed in the United States of America
04 05 06 07 08 DELTA 9 8 7 6 5 4 3 2 1

Contents

Acknowledgments

The publishers wish to thank Tim Clinton and Doris Rikkers for their creative and editorial contributions to this project.

Introduction

Mary stood outside the tomb crying. . . . She turned around and saw Jesus standing there, but she did not realize that it was Jesus. . . .

Jesus said to her, "Mary."

She turned toward him and cried out in Aramaic, "Rabboni!" (which means Teacher).

Jesus said, "Do not hold on to me, for I have not yet returned to the Father. Go instead to my brothers and tell them, 'I am returning to my Father and your Father, to my God and your God.'"

—*JOHN 20:11, 14, 16–17*

What a wonderful and amazing God we have! With just one word, Jesus changed everything for Mary. He quietly and gently said her name. Once devastated by disappointment, anger, and grief, Mary was now restored to ecstatic joy—her friend, her teacher, her Lord was alive! Her world was changed and her life had a new outlook all because of one word, and in that one word Mary knew Jesus cared deeply about her and loved her.

God knows each of you and cares for you just as He cared about Mary. He knows your name; you belong to Him (Isaiah 43:1). No matter who you are or what kind of baggage you carry with you, no matter what you look like or feel like, no matter what you do or don't do, God loves you just as you are right now. You don't have to get your act together, lose ten pounds, run a marathon, write a best-selling book, or raise perfect children. You are an extraordinary woman in His sight right now.

Not only does He love you, He cherishes you. He wants to have a close, loving relationship with you like no one on earth can. All you have to do is make yourself open and available to spend time with Him and feel His loving arms encircle you.

We invite you now to read these chapters and come to a closer and more loving relationship with our wonderful, awesome, and loving God who is here for you.

A Woman and Her God

A Woman and Her God

❧

BETH MOORE

What does the LORD require of you?
To act justly and to love mercy
and to walk humbly with your God.

—MICAH 6:8

I think I have discovered what makes life work. Test me on this and see if it is true. In this chapter, we will look at two scriptures and compare them. Within these verses, we'll uncover the secret to what makes life work.

Deuteronomy 7:7–8 says, "The LORD did not set his

affection on you and choose you because you were more numerous than other peoples, for you were the fewest of all peoples. But it was because the LORD loved you." A truth about our God is that He is the same yesterday, today, and forever. The New Testament tells us that God loves believers in Christ the same way He loved His people in the Old Testament. We also know that we have been chosen in Christ for God. We need to claim these things personally. Don't think of His love in a corporate manner—a sanctuary packed with people or a throne surrounded by thousands and thousands of believers. For now, consider how God feels about *you*. The Word of God says that He is holy, most righteous, most perfect, full of splendor—He is a God who has set His affections on *you*.

Keep in mind that Deuteronomy tells us that God did not set His affections on us because we were many in number or talented or had anything to offer Him, but because He loved us. Colossians 3:1–4 says, "Since, then, you have been raised with Christ, set your hearts on things above, where Christ is seated at the right hand of God. Set your minds on things above, not on earthly things. For you died, and your life is now hidden with Christ in God. When Christ, who is your life, appears, then you also will appear with him in glory." Deuteronomy and Colossians tell us that God created us and set His affections upon us; we were chosen in Him. In return, He asks us to set our affections upon Him.

Therefore, life works most perfectly when a reciprocal love relationship is in place between man and God. This does not guarantee an easy life or one without suffering; but when we seek to glorify God in all that we do, His love will carry us through any hardship. It is then that you can say, "I may not understand what God is doing in my life right now, but I know He loves me." Our relationship with Him will eclipse everything else in our lives.

If it's true that His love must become to us better than life, consider how King David, a man after God's own heart, viewed God. If you looked for the very heart of God's Word, you needn't look any further than David's words expressed in Psalm 63. This psalm is the heart of an intimate relationship that God initiated in Genesis 1 and finalized at the wedding supper of the Lamb in Revelation 19.

O God, you are my God,

 earnestly I seek you;

my soul thirsts for you,

 my body longs for you,

in a dry and weary land

 where there is no water.

I have seen you in the sanctuary

 and beheld your power and your glory.

Because your love is better than life,

 my lips will glorify you.

I will praise you as long as I live,

 and in your name I will lift up my hands.

My soul will be satisfied as with the richest of foods;

 with singing lips my mouth will praise you.

On my bed I remember you;

 I think of you through the watches of the night.

Because you are my help,

 I sing in the shadow of your wings.

My soul clings to you;

 your right hand upholds me.

They who seek my life will be destroyed;

    they will go down to the depths of the earth.

They will be given over to the sword

    and become food for jackals.

But the king will rejoice in God;

    all who swear by God's name will praise him,

    while the mouths of liars will be silenced. (Psalm 63)

I pray that as you read those words, you saw not only with your eyes, but also with your heart. This description is the sacred romance that each one of us is meant to encounter with God. It describes the purpose of our existence. Consider again the first few words: "O God, you are my God." Is that something that you can say? Have you encountered Him in such a way that He has become your refuge and strength? "O God of all the universe, who called the worlds into being, You are mine."

This is a psalm about intimacy and the relationship that we were born to enjoy with God. It is a psalm of prayer and devotion, prompted by the heart. Many people are motivated by discipline. Discipline is getting up and having a time of prayer and devotion with God when we are weary from exhaustion. On a daily basis, however, our heart should yearn to be with Him, as well as our soul. Our longing and thirsting comes as a gift from the Holy Spirit, and we desire it more than life. The heart of this psalm says, "Give me a thirst and a hunger for You, God. Not just a discipline. Give me an ache and a longing to know You, to be with You, to abide in You always."

Psalm 63:3 says, "Your love is better than life." Can you say today, by faith and conviction, that His love is better to you than life? I wonder what circumstances helped you see that there is nothing in life that can truly satisfy outside of Him. There are wonderful things that affect us, but nothing can touch us at the depth that God can touch us.

Psalm 63 also refers to the transcendence of God, which means that absolutely nothing compares to Him. The most wonderful things on earth fade in the distance in comparison with Him. He wants us to come to a point in our relationship with Him where we can say, "You are so far above and beyond every other thing in my life, every other love in my life, every other experience in my life, every other purpose or goal in my life. You *are* my life. Not just the most important thing in my life—You are my life. And Your love, God, is better than life. In fact, Lord, I lay down my life today to see You face to face because You are better than life." We were meant to utterly devote ourselves to Him.

SEEKING SATISFACTION

Look again at Psalm 63:5: "My soul will be satisfied as with the richest of foods." Spiritually speaking, a relationship with God is like feeding our souls with rich, luscious foods. We were never meant to go on a spiritual diet. We don't have to be lean with God. This is one area of our life where we can be lavish. Our souls were created to feast on Him. Do you feast on the Lord? Do you have a soul that is satisfied? I know the difference between a spiritual feast and a spiritual famine, and I want you to savor the bounty of God's riches. That's what King David refers to. We were created to crave this

God made our souls to long for Him, and we are not fully satisfied without His presence in our lives.

relationship. God made our souls to long for Him, and we are not fully satisfied without His presence in our lives.

However, we can believe in Christ and know Him for years but still not possess a satisfied soul. Salvation does not equal satisfaction. We receive salvation, but we seek satisfaction. The Word says to be filled with Him. We may actively pursue this and want it more than anything else in our lives, but satisfaction is a different matter.

Often believers will live for years ignoring their secret ache. They don't want to admit to anybody that their souls are empty and something inside aches to be satisfied. Oftentimes we mistakenly assume that our need can be met out in the world, but it can't. We make the mistake of never letting Him fill our lives on a daily basis and become our soul's richest food. This is the essence of the sacred romance. Christ wants to romance our soul.

The Unsatisfied Soul

An unsatisfied soul is an accident waiting to happen. Consider the saying, "Nature abhors a vacuum." Human nature also abhors a vacuum. In other words, we avoid feeling empty and always find ways to fill it. God created that void so we would seek Him. We are not satisfied by simply accepting salvation and then ascending to heaven when the time comes. Instead, God wants us to have a relationship with Him during our lifetime. When we don't, we set ourselves up for disaster. If we don't find satisfaction with God, we will look for it somewhere else. When we do, we default to one of two things: subsistence living or substitute living.

Consider the word *subsistence*. One definition of the helpless is that they are poor and needy, "subsisting on the alms of others." The picture painted here is a beggar. If we subsist on the alms of others, our heart is just a vacuum; we're needy people because we were created that way. We need to be loved. We need to be affirmed. Those are not weaknesses. We were created with those needs, and we are like beggars when our soul is not satisfied by God. It's like we walk around all day with an empty cup, asking people to fill it up. We may go to our spouse, our children, our friends. We may even ask our coworkers, neighbors, and pastor, "Can you fill my cup?" The problem is that we go to them seeking what only Christ was meant to provide. We can affirm one another, even fulfill one another, but it was God's design right from the beginning that He alone would satisfy our soul's desire. We were meant to thrive on the riches of His love. We were never meant for subsistence living.

One other method of coping without Christ is substitute living. In Isaiah 44:20, the prophet is inspired by God to describe what happens when we fall into idolatry. (Idolatry, of course, is anything we worship or bow down to aside from God.) Consider the state of man in Isaiah 44:20: "He feeds on ashes, a deluded heart misleads him." The Word of God tells us in the Book of Jeremiah that our heart is deceitful above all things. When our heart is not fully given to Christ, we can't even trust what we're feeling or what our heart is telling us.

The world tells us we should follow our heart, but sometimes we follow it into all sorts of traps. Scripture admonishes us, "A deluded heart misleads him; he cannot save himself, or say, 'Is not this thing in my right hand a lie?'" (Isaiah 44:20). What is "a lie"? It's anything we hold onto for strength, might, comfort, or security. It can be a number of things: work, food, alcohol, drugs, power, and money. Any attempted identity outside of Christ is a lie. Our cravings are a good indication of what a lie is. To crave something outside of God and never feel like we have enough is a deluded heart misleading us. If there is anything you're clinging to except the love of God, I pray you'll redirect your vision to the one and only God. Remember, what you are holding onto will betray you every time if it isn't from God.

Food That Satisfies

The Word of God is health and life not only to our soul, but also to the marrow of our bones. God has taught me that His Word is alive and powerful. When someone shares a verse from His Word, God prompts me to actively incorporate it into my thoughts. I don't just read it; I ask God to make it abide within me.

Psalm 90:14 says, "Satisfy us in the morning with your unfailing love, that we may sing for joy and be glad all our days." This speaks of satisfaction. We can't just decide, "Lord, I want to be satisfied with You for the rest of my days. I want to know the kind of love that is better than life. And I ask You, Lord, to give it to me today," and then expect that our needs will be met until we see Him face to face. Our needs are a daily concern. We wake up every day and have new ones. We need to feel like we're significant to someone. Most importantly, we need to feel like we are loved that day.

Long before my family wakes up in my house and before I expect them to meet a need I might have, God has taught me to go to Him. During that time I pour out my heart, confessing sins that have built up in my life since the previous day. There's rarely a day that I don't have something to confess. The closer and closer we grow to Him, the pickier He gets. And He begins to talk to us, show us, and convict us about our attitude and motives, such as things we were thinking about doing but eventually avoided because we did not want to take the time to minister to someone. So when I ask the Holy Spirit to shed light on my sins over the last twenty-four hours, He always reveals something. Maybe a missed opportunity to enjoy His presence the day before or simply not spending enough time with Him. Maybe I spent a full hour in the car yesterday, and rather than spending it with Him or enjoying the beauty He provides in the way of a sunset, I listened to the radio.

Psalm 62 tells us that we can pour out our heart to God. He is a refuge for us. This is a good opportunity to remove from our "cup" anything that is a false comfort. For example, a problem arises—maybe someone close to us has mishandled a situation—we tattle to God. Or somebody hurts us and we simply need to turn the other cheek. We go to God first and say, "I want You to know something. That person really hurt my feelings. But in Your name, I'm going to do what You would want me to do here. And I need You to minister to me so that I can handle this properly." In that way we're pouring out our heart in order to make room for Him because He wants to fill our heart with His love. You see, if we're already full of ourselves—full of our own anxieties and concerns— we don't have very much room for Him. So it's very important that we start our day by pouring out our needs to the Lord, allowing Him to meet them, rather than looking for others to have to satisfy that need. In that way, we are really ready to start the day with a servant's heart.

When we've followed through with this, it's as if we're

saying to Him, "Lord, You know me. You know my natural personality is given to fear. You know all my insecurities. You know that I have a need to be loved and to feel significant and to feel affirmed. And Father, I'm not going to ask my family to do that for me today. They may or may not, and if they do, that's wonderful. But Father, You are my sole satisfaction, and I ask You to satisfy me this morning with Your unfailing love."

The Bible repeatedly speaks of unfailing love, referring to God's love. His is the only love that never fails. Fortunately, it's not based on how well we lived our last twenty-four hours or how much we obeyed Him. His love is unconditional. He is completely biased. He cannot strip Himself of His Fatherhood to us in order to make an unbiased decision about us. And so we go to Him and ask Him, "Satisfy me, Lord. Not with crumbs under the table, but from the feast You've prepared for my soul." We were not asked to be beggars for God. We were not asked to sit outside the door and hold out a cup for scraps. I'm not referring to a prosperity gospel. If I were, I'd say, "Lord, give me things." But we don't want things; we want our heavenly Father.

So we pray to Him, "Lord, You're what I want. You are what I long for. You are the great reward. I want the fullness of You in my life. Not just what You can give me. I want You. I want You." As we begin to approach Him like that and we ask Him to rid us of the lesser gods in our lives, He'll not only fill that cup, He will overflow it. One thing that is so incredible about allowing our Father to meet our needs first thing in the day is that if our husband or friend showers us with love later on, our cup overflows. But it's not their job to initially meet the needs of our soul. Therefore, they enjoy the delight (and so do we) of causing this wonderful overflow. And what a difference that makes!

Not long ago, during my prayer time, God put it upon my heart to call my husband. But God didn't want me to call him on his cell phone as he was driving to work. Instead, my call was going to be a message for him when he arrived. And my message was going to be to tell him that I loved him more than any earthly thing, that he was so important to me, and that he was doing an incredible job. And so I walked to the phone and dialed his number. And this is what I told him: "I just want you to know before you hit the hardships of the day and no matter what kind of day this becomes, I want you to know before anyone complains to you, that I love you with all my heart and you are such a wonderful husband and I think you're talented and I think you're smart." And being funny is big in our house so I had to say, "And I think you're the funniest person I've ever known in all my life." God had encouraged me to really shower him with praise, and then I just hung up the phone.

And when I returned to my devotional time, I thought it was peculiar that God had called me to do this in the middle of devotions. And then He told me, *Do you realize that's exactly what I want to do with My children?* You see, life's hard. We may get some affirmation during the course of the day, but in some workplaces people receive very little edifying. And family situations may not be particularly healthy or encouraging. But our message from God each and every day is, "Child, you are tremendously significant to Me. You are everything to Me." Christ says, "I laid down My life. Your love to Me, child, is better than My life." Do you understand what He's saying? Loving you was better than sparing Christ's life. And He wants to tell you these things before anybody else begins to tear away at you during the course of the day, before you are worn and torn by the interactions and activities of the next twenty-four hours.

He wants to satisfy your soul with His unfailing love and say, "Child, you are everything to Me. Be full of My love today, full of My Spirit today. You are so important." Jehovah God, who spoke the world into being, thinks that your life is better than His Son's. That's why He laid down His life for you, so that you could be free to know a love that is better than life. I want you to understand how significant that is. "O God, you are my God." No wonder the psalmist said, "Earnestly I seek you." Not just out of discipline, but because that's what he longed for more than anything else in life—to be connected to his God. "Because your love is better than life, my lips shall glorify you. . . . My soul shall be satisfied as with the richest of foods."

> He wants to satisfy your soul with His unfailing love and say, "Child, you are everything to Me."

PRAYER

Oh, Father, how we praise You. How we thank You that You did not call us to subsistence living. We don't have to live on the alms of others. You had more in mind for us than that. We don't have to seek some other means of satisfaction or a substitute that never fulfills us. I pray that today we can look in our right hand and say, "This is a lie if it's not from You." Father, help us to loosen our grip on the things that we crave so much in life, the things that we want affirmation and approval from so desperately. Help us to release our grip on them and hang onto You instead, because Your love is better than life. In the sweetest name I know, the name of Jesus, amen.

ABOUT THE AUTHOR

Beth Moore is the best-selling, award-winning author of *Things Pondered, A Heart Like His,* and *Praying God's Word.* She is a noted international conference speaker, teacher, and writer of highly acclaimed women's Bible studies and devotionals. Beth is the founder of the ministry Living Proof, as well as a Sunday school teacher at First Baptist Church in Houston, Texas. She holds a B.S. degree from Southwest Texas State University.

Verses That Inspire

Let us draw near to God with a sincere heart in full assurance of faith, having our hearts sprinkled to cleanse us from a guilty conscience and having our bodies washed with pure water. Let us hold unswervingly to the hope we profess, for he who promised is faithful. (Hebrews 10:22–23)

We know and rely on the love God has for us. (1 John 4:16)

Teach me to do your will,
for you are my God;
may your good Spirit
lead me on level ground. (Psalm 143:10)

Let all who take refuge in you be glad;

    let them ever sing for joy.

Spread your protection over them,

    that those who love your name may rejoice in you.

For surely, O LORD, you bless the righteous;

    you surround them with your favor as with a shield.

    (Psalm 5:11–12)

A Woman's Role: Ministering Like Jesus

⚜

JILL BRISCOE

The Lord is full of compassion and mercy.

—JAMES 5:11

What is a woman's role today? This is an issue debated far and wide in the church. What can women do, what can't we do, what should we do, what could we do, and what would we do? That is the question: Where is our place? Let's turn to the Scriptures for our answers.

Jesus' Heart for Women

The Bible makes it very clear that Jesus had a heart for women. Women were the first ones to appear at the foot of His cross and the last ones to leave. They were also the first to be sent by Jesus to tell the men about His resurrection. And throughout the Bible, women are valid witnesses for the truth about Jesus.

Interestingly enough, Jesus ignored many rabbinical rules concerning women. His attitude toward women opened the way for them to be welcomed and involved in His ministry. When John, who lived with Jesus and followed Him for three years, wanted to write an account of Jesus' life, he looked back over the incidents he had witnessed and heard about and included only those that were most important to Jesus' ministry. And it is incredible to see how many stories about women are in his Gospel. Luke's account also reveals numerous incidences with women, but in the Gospel of John we learn about the woman at the well.

In Jesus' day, women were not treated with respect. They were considered along the same lines as a slave or child in that they were seen as property. That was the thinking of the day. The rabbis especially treated women unkindly. They considered women unclean because of their monthly periods; therefore women were prohibited from worshiping in certain parts of the temple because they might defile it. It came as a surprise, then, when Jesus invited the Samaritan woman to worship. In fact, He instructed her about how to worship. Jesus disregarded all sorts of rabbinical teachings of His day through His example, His teaching, His attitude, and His miracles.

Jesus also allowed women to touch Him. This was just not allowed. A woman was *never* allowed to come in contact with a rabbi. Do you remember the woman who touched the hem of His garment (Luke 8:40–48)? Jesus immediately turned around and said, "Who touched me?" But He did not rebuke her, as the rabbis would have done. Instead, He hailed her. In fact, He held her up as an example of faith. Jesus often reached out to women, which would make other rabbis cringe in horror.

Do you remember the widow of Nain who had only one son, and when he died she went out to bury him (Luke 7:11–17)? Jesus met the funeral procession and touched the bier where the dead man was lying. This was absolutely incredible to the Jews who were there. Surely Jesus had defiled Himself by touching a dead body. But His touch resurrected the young man. When Jesus first met the widow, she was mourning. (This was, after all, her only son and she might now become destitute.) Jesus simply said to her, "Don't cry." What does this comment tell us about Jesus' heart? He cared for women. He cared for this widow, and He cared for her dead son. He touched the dead and they arose. He was life; He was resurrection.

Jesus also talked to women. On one occasion He describes a woman as "daughter of Abraham" (Luke 13:16). The Pharisees standing nearby must have said, "Sons of Abraham, yes, but daughters of Abraham? What is this? This is new teaching."

Jesus' example, then, shows us He touched women, He talked to women, and He taught women. Remember Mary and Martha (Luke 10:38–42)? Martha became distracted by her need to serve. That's easy to do for us women. We become more enamored "by the work of the Lord rather than the Lord of the work!" And Martha was busy. She allowed her distractions to occupy her thoughts, and she forgot all about being attentive to the Lord. But in Jesus' day, rabbis didn't take time to teach a woman. "Better to give the toy to a dog than a woman," they would say. But in this instance, Jesus rebuked Martha for not recognizing what is important. With respect to Mary He said, "She's sitting at My feet and she's listening to My Word, and that's very, very important." And so here is an example of a rabbi teaching a woman. This was absolutely revolutionary. Jesus simply ignored people's views of women and said, "This is what I think about women. I have a heart for them. They shall not be excluded from My kingdom."

Jesus simply ignored people's views of women and said, "This is what I think about women. I have a heart for them. They shall not be excluded from My kingdom."

PARABLES OF WOMEN

Many of the parables of the New Testament also incorporate women as examples. This must have been a real eye-opener for the people listening to Jesus. Jesus presented one-third of all His teaching in parable form, and He was the first person to put women into those stories. He wanted them to know His feelings, thoughts, and attitudes about women.

In the parable about the obstinate widow and the harsh judge (Luke 18:1–8) the widow is the positive figure, while the judge is the negative one. This is a parable about prayer, and as with many of the parables, it has a twin. The other parable concerns a sinner who is praying in the temple. Jesus' point is: Pray persistently and with humility, and be repentant. He uses both male and female figures in His stories to convey His point.

The parable of the lost coin (Luke 15:8–10) is part of the wonderful trilogy of the "lost" parables: the lost son, the lost coin, and the lost sheep. Incredibly, Jesus uses a woman as an analogy to Himself! She is searching for a lost coin, just as God Himself seeks the lost. This illustration certainly must have surprised the Jews listening to Jesus' stories, but He made His point.

Another example can be found in Matthew 13 in the parable of the leaven and the dough. Jesus refers to a woman who's kneading dough. The women in His audience must have been thrilled to hear such an illustration! Can you imagine sitting in church all your life, hearing sermons that never relate to you? Then suddenly, a wonderful teacher emerges who regularly uses women in His stories.

THE SAMARITAN WOMAN

Let's look at the story in John 4 where Jesus meets the Samaritan woman—the woman at the well. This is a woman who had two strikes against her, but Jesus uses her as a witness after she comes to faith in Him. In fact, she brings her whole town to Jesus Christ.

I want you to see this story in a little different light. Jesus was tired. It had been a long, hot, dusty walk. Not as long as it might have been, however, if He had traveled around Samaria, as other Jews did, rather than through it. It had been an executive decision, certainly not the team's call. They arrived at the well outside Sychar just before lunch.

"Great," grumbled Peter. "Now we're going to have to buy lunch from the Samaritans." Grim-faced, they left Jesus sitting on the ancient well that Jacob had dug for his fore-fathers and set off down the dusty hill. But Jesus was thirsty from the long walk. It might have seemed a little frustrating to be sitting on a well without a bucket, although He who made the rivers and lakes could have cared for His needs. Jesus had the power to turn stone to bread or sand to water, but He did not have the permission. His Father hadn't granted it. God wanted His beloved Son to endure a period of depri-vation for the good of the kingdom. So Jesus batted away the flies that buzzed around His face and He looked toward the village. At that moment He saw the lone figure of a woman balancing a water jug on her head as she climbed the long hill toward Him. And suddenly He knew without a shadow of a doubt why He'd been determined to travel through Samaria. "She's coming home, Father!" He must have shouted. "She's coming home."

The Samaritan woman said, in effect, "You're a Jew, and you're asking me, a Samaritan, for a drink?" In those days, Jews never put their lips to a vessel from which a Gentile had drunk. And not only a Gentile, but a Samaritan Gentile. And not only a Samaritan Gentile, but a woman! But Jesus said,

"Give Me a drink from your jug." No wonder the woman was startled! In this passage of Scripture, Jesus talks to the woman about water. He says to her, "If you only knew who you are talking to, you would ask Me and I would give you living water." And the words He used meant "a spring of water," an "artesian well."

I have personal experience with an artesian well. My husband and I live in Wisconsin in a charming, renovated 1840s schoolhouse next to a little lake. I was concerned about the lake when we first moved there because it's so weedy. It's ideal as a fishing lake, but I wondered if the weeds would overtake the water. So I arranged a meeting with my neighbors and started a lake association. A man from the water bureau came out and talked to all of us about weeds and reeds and things like that.

Then he turned to me and said, "You know, you don't need to be worried about your lake. It's an artesian lake."

Remembering that word from the Bible, I said, "What's that? Tell me about it."

"Have you noticed squiggly things in the water?" he asked me.

"Yes! It looks like spaghetti."

"Well, that's the small water springs," he explained. "This lake is like a sieve."

Weeds and reeds will never choke my lake because it's an artesian well. Jesus looked at the Samaritan woman and said, "You are thirsty, woman. You've obviously been drinking at the wrong well. If you knew who you are talking to, you would ask Me and I would give you Living Water. Water that springs up like an artesian well so you will never be thirsty again." This woman not only met a man at the well, she met a man who offered her something she desperately needed.

All of us know women who are thirsty. They are drinking from wells that are cracked, as the Old Testament says, drinking from cisterns that cannot hold water because they're cracked and broken (Jeremiah 2:13). We know people like that, who look for meaning in their life through relationships. The Samaritan woman had had five men in her life, four husbands and one she was not married to. Other people may choose to drink from the well of religion. They try to satisfy their thirst by adhering to dry, cold, hard rules and good works. Some people drink from the well of fitness or the well of success or family. You can drink from all sorts of wells, but unless the source of your water is the Living Water Himself, you will never be satisfied.

I come from a well-off family in Britain. And until the latter part of their lives, my family did not know Christ as I know Him now. I was brought up without knowing God in Christ, and

You can drink from all sorts of wells, but unless the source of your water is the Living Water Himself, you will never be satisfied.

without hope; yet they are a wonderful family. I accepted Christ, entered the mission field, and lived in a tiny cottage in a youth center where my husband and I served for ten years in Britain and Europe. My mom had two beautiful homes, one in Liverpool and a country home in the lake district. When my parents traveled from their Liverpool home to their country home, they would stop at our cottage and visit us. One time, as my mom was preparing to leave us to go to her country manor, she hesitated. She didn't want to leave.

"Jill, God lives here, doesn't He?" she said.

I took a deep breath and said, "Yes, Mom, He does. And I'd rather live in my cottage with Jesus than a castle without

Him." Only Christ can offer true satisfaction. No other well can equal the Living Water He offers us.

VISION, PASSION, MISSION

Jesus also had a vision, a passion, and a mission. Those are the three words I want us to consider, because women can be involved in a ministry with vision, a passion, and a mission. Once again, consider Jesus and this Samaritan woman. God delighted in taking the least, the lost, and the last—like this woman—and using them. How quickly did the Samaritan woman understand His heart, His purpose, and His mission! The woman at the well, I believe, represents women every-where—women who are forgiven sinners and women who are unforgiven sinners. Which describes you? The Samaritan woman was unforgiven, just like a lot of women in the world. But then she encountered Jesus.

I have the privilege of serving World Relief, an organiza-tion that assists people in need. I am also invited to speak all over the world and so I travel around the globe probably once a year. I meet a lot of women. And I am overwhelmed by the response of women to the gospel, the good news that Jesus came to seek and to save those who are lost. Men and women are equally lost and can be equally saved. Lost people who've been given gifts to be used for kingdom work—to serve Jesus and to serve others.

So the Samaritan woman is about to have grace enter her life through this man at the well, this man who sees her need. Even though He is thirsty and hungry and tired, when He meets her, His passion and vision for a lost soul take center stage. And where are the disciples at this time? I think they represent church people. They are disciples of Jesus, convinced He's the Messiah, having left everything to follow Him; but they are mostly focused on their lunch. They represent us, quite honestly. They can't take their eyes off material possessions and focus on spiritual realities, including things God has asked them to do in this world. So they've walked into town to buy bread. When the disciples return, they're surprised to find Jesus talking to a Samaritan woman. Finally, she departs, leaving her water jug with Jesus. At this point, the disciples offer Him lunch.

"Rabbi, eat something," they say.

"I have food to eat you don't know anything about," He explains.

"Did somebody bring Him lunch?" they ask, looking around. "Did He eat her lunch? Well, who brought Him lunch?" How frustrated He must have been with the disciples! For that matter, how frustrated He must be with us when we can't take our focus off lunch. Our vision is so limited. The problem is, if we become comfortable in our faith, we tend to become self-satisfied and then we don't even care if the world's gone to hell in a handbasket. We have no vision and certainly no passion.

But Jesus had a driving passion for the harvest fields. Look at John 4:35: "Open your eyes and look at the fields! They are ripe for harvest." What was He looking at just then? He was looking down the hill toward the village. He was seeing all the villagers coming to Him in their long, white robes, winding their way up the hill. And they must have looked like sheaves of wheat walking. And Jesus said, "Look, open your eyes. Look at the fields ready for harvest. How can you think of food at a time like this?"

If you have a vision for the lost, you tend to lose your

appetite, because your vision leads to passion. Suddenly your stomach becomes tied in knots. Let me ask you something: When was the last time your stomach ached over a lost soul? Take a good look at the people around you. Just as it was in biblical times, the fields are ripe. It's harvest time! Proverbs 10:5 says a son who sleeps during a harvest is a disgrace to his father. Remember, the harvest field is ripe. Certainly in America there are sheaves all over the place, thirsty sheaves longing for a drink of Living Water, not knowing even how to ask for it. "Gather me into God's barn," their souls cry out. But we are so focused on our own lives, we can't take our eyes off our lunch.

Meanwhile, Jesus was driven to do the will of God as revealed in the Word of God. When we're intent on doing the will of God and fulfilling His purpose for our lives, then we are going to discover His will. And His will is revealed in the Word of God. It's right there, for you and me. God's plan for our lives is to come alongside those who do not know Him. That's a privilege. It's exciting! But remember, He also said, "The night comes when no man can work" (John 9:4). He finished His work. Night came. Now we must finish ours.

A HEART FOR THE LOST

So how do you foster a heart for the lost? First of all, you have to develop a sense of lostness. When I first became a Christian, I was a student at a college in Cambridge, England. I had no Christian background. I was five years old during World War II, and I decided that if God was indeed in heaven, then He wasn't very nice or clever or good, because He couldn't stop the bombs dropping all about me. And I grew up believing that. And then I went to college, and for the first time in my life I met people who believed in a God—a God who was real and a Christ who was God. This was an extraordinary revelation to me! Here I was in the midst of very clever students, good-looking and fine athletes, and they believed these incredible things. They embraced a Christian belief system and affirmed a Christian creed. And they told me about the Lord.

At this time, it was all I could do to grapple with the concept of God. Then I was given a concept of lostness, which was really a mind-blowing experience. The first Christian book I ever read was C. S. Lewis's *The Screwtape Letters,* which is the journal of a senior devil to a junior devil. C. S. Lewis happened to be a professor at Cambridge while I was there, and he was a very prominent man. So I thought, *Here is an incredible, brilliant person who believes in lostness and the devil. How can this be?* I felt compelled to investigate the Christian faith.

Then I became sick, was taken to the hospital, and the girl in the next bed led me thoroughly, totally, irrevocably to Jesus Christ. I've never been the same. Yet I couldn't have met the One who offered me Living Water if I hadn't believed in lostness. I would not have felt the need to be saved. The girl who led me to Christ made sure that I understood and acknowledged that concept. Jesus believes in lostness. It does not matter whether you're Presbyterian, Methodist, Catholic, or Baptist. There are lost Baptists and there are saved Baptists. Just because you attend a worship service in a building doesn't make you a Christian. Like Billy Graham once said, "You can be born in a garage, but it doesn't make you a car."

So Jesus said to the Samaritan woman, "You're lost. Salvation is from the Jews. I have the words of eternal life. Listen to Me and you will live." He explained to her many things in a very short time, and she came to faith. Unlike His disciples, Jesus believed that this woman—and all women—could come to faith. He even believed that a woman like me—an arrogant, self-sufficient student rushing around Cambridge, speaking with great authority from the depths of my considerable ignorance about nothing very much—could one day believe in Him. His heart ached for me, just as it did for this woman. But it will only work if we believe in lostness. And if we understand this concept and how we came to faith, then it will transform our lives. And this is why: When we look around and see our mother, who is lost, and

We're going to have to put on our global glasses if we ever hope to spread the gospel to the lost.

our sister and our friend and our boss and our colleagues, we're going to want to do something about it. But we're going to have to put on our global glasses if we ever hope to successfully spread the gospel to the lost. This is our Father's world that broke our Father's heart, but our Father wants it back and He's going to use us to do it.

DOING HOMEWORK TO REACH THE LOST

So how are we going to reach the lost? We've got to do our homework. Jesus did His when He talked to the Samaritan woman. Naturally, He knew her background, since Samaritans and Jews had once shared a common heritage. But when the Babylonians came and carted the Jews off to Babylon, they left a few behind. The few who were left behind married heathen people. They had children and became a group of part-Jew, part-heathen people known as Samaritans. Orthodox Jews despised Samaritans because they were a "mongrel" race. They weren't maintaining all the Jewish laws. And so they became confused about where to worship. Should they worship at Mount Gerizim or at the temple in Jerusalem?

But Jesus ignores the Samaritan woman's comment about where to worship (John 4:19–20). Instead, He focuses on her beliefs and her background. He uses this information as a bridge rather than a barrier. He says, "It isn't where you worship and it isn't how you worship; it's who you worship that matters. And you must worship in spirit and in truth. In reality, you can do it. Yes, you're a woman. Yes, you're a

Samaritan woman. Yes, you're a despised woman. Yes, you've made wrong choices. Yes, you're a sinful woman. But I am inviting you to worship Me." Now, if anything stirs a woman's heart, it's that kind of invitation. "I want you to worship Me. There's a place beside Me for you." Jesus was wearing His global glasses, and He'd done His homework.

If we are going to reach women for Christ and teach women for Christ, then we're going to have to examine our contemporary culture and determine where women are, how they think, what they do, where they go, and how they dress. What makes up a woman's world? Do we understand it? Have we done our homework?

Thirty years ago, when I first started to reach out to women through a women's ministry program, there was simply one group of women. I started a Bible study with six women and it eventually grew to eight hundred. I stood up, taught the Scriptures, and then went home. But things have changed. You have to do your homework. Women are more like tribes now. There's a tribe of young mothers, there's a tribe of widows, there's a tribe of women who work outside the home, and there's a tribe of divorced women. Each tribe has its own culture, language, dress, thought process, and needs. What attracts a young mother will not necessarily attract a widow or a divorced woman. To reach women, we often have to understand their contemporary culture. For example, what is life like for a divorced woman who feels rejected? And do we understand the young mother who is happily married, trying to raise godly children? She is a world apart from the divorced woman. We have to do our homework if we're ever going to reach the lost.

And this is what Jesus did with the woman at the well. He knew what to say, and He knew how to say it. His vision led to passion. "Oh, if you only knew," He said. And eventually she did. And this led to a mission. What else would you call it when the Samaritan woman won a city to Christ? She was a brand-new believer. Do you have to attend a seminary or Bible college before you can win your whole town to Christ? Absolutely not! You can start as soon as you believe.

When the girl in the hospital bed next to me led me to Christ, she said, "Now, Jill, everybody who comes to your bedside is going to hear what you did today."

"They are?" I asked.

"Yes," she said.

"Who's going to tell them?"

"You are."

"What do I tell them?"

"Tell them what you just did. Tell them about our conversation."

"Who am I going to tell?" I asked.

"Everybody who comes to your bedside. Look! There's a nurse coming. Start with her."

And so I did. And that day there were not a few people who heard me explain in a stumbling, awkward manner who Christ is.

Now it's your turn. You are a woman who Jesus loves and calls to minister to the lost. Start your ministry. Just start right where you are. The mission field is literally between your own two feet at any given time.

About the Author

Jill Briscoe is author of over forty books. She and her husband are Ministers at Large of Elmbrook Church in Wisconsin. She is also executive editor of the women's magazine *Just Between Us* for women in leadership, and serves on the boards of World Relief and Christianity Today International. She also ministers globally and with Telling the Truth media ministries.

Verses That Inspire

Let us not become weary in doing good, for at the proper time we will reap a harvest if we do not give up. (Galatians 6:9)

Stand firm. Let nothing move you. Always give yourselves fully to the work of the Lord, because you know that your labor in the Lord is not in vain. (1 Corinthians 15:58)

The Sovereign LORD has given me an instructed tongue, to know the word that sustains the weary. (Isaiah 50:4)

We are God's workmanship, created in Christ Jesus to do good works, which God prepared in advance for us to do. (Ephesians 2:10)

Transforming Your Self-Concept

❧

SANDRA D. WILSON

The LORD says . . . "I have summoned you
by name; you are mine."

—ISAIAH 43:1

Do you know who you are?

Initially that's an amusing question. But it's also a thought-provoking question, and a question I want you to consider: Do you know who you are? How do we determine who we are? How do we develop our self-concept, and what difference does it make in our lives as daughters of the Lord?

As friends? As daughters of earthly parents? Perhaps as a sister, as a wife, as a mother? What difference does it make? As you will see, it makes a very big difference. Let's explore this idea of developing our self-concept.

ESTABLISHING A SELF-CONCEPT

I have never met my biological father. I sometimes consider myself semilegitimate, because my mother thought she was married when I was conceived. When she met my father, she fell head over heels in love and they married within a couple of months of meeting one another. Unfortunately, she failed to find out some important things. For example, he was already married. He had never bothered with a divorce; he just moved away.

When my mother discovered she was pregnant, she was thrilled. My father was not. She couldn't understand why he insisted she have an abortion. My mother made it clear to him that she wanted this child and would never consider an abortion.

She told me that when my father realized she wasn't

going to have an abortion, he tried to kill her in what would have looked like a gun-cleaning accident. About that time, federal authorities caught up with him because he wasn't just a bigamist, but also an embezzler. Since his crime involved the U.S. Postal Service, his misdeed was a federal offense. At this point my mother was in Arizona, three thousand miles from her family in New England, giving birth to a fatherless child decades before that ever became "fashionable."

My mother felt it was best for me to have a father, so she remarried when I was two. Again, she did it rather hastily and there was something very important about this man she didn't know: He had been an alcoholic for years. If you have lived with this problem you know all too well the chaos alcoholism brings into a family. It distorts a child's self-concept. It's similar to looking into a fun house mirror. It's definitely distorted, but there's not much fun in a dysfunctional family. I lived under the burden of unrealistic expectations common to the first child in an alcoholic family. And I also experienced several isolated episodes of sexual abuse, the most profound of which I totally blocked out from my memory for over thirty years.

All of these experiences worked together to create in me a sense that no matter what I did, it wasn't good enough. That no matter how hard I worked, I should try harder. I really believed that I was supposed to be a perfect person.

Sadly, I carried my erroneous and painful perceptions into adulthood—as all children do. And when we've experienced neglect or abuse in childhood, we usually struggle as adults with a sense that there is something terribly, even *uniquely,* wrong with us. We may believe we are flawed in a way that others never could be. We even think that we are less worthy than others. For years I've referred to this as "unbiblical shame." Why "unbiblical"? Clearly God's Word states that everyone is flawed by sin. So no one is uniquely flawed. I cannot be worth less than another person, because we are all damaged by sin, according to God's Word.

Flawed! It's so painful living with this knowledge about yourself. You feel like you're a great disappointment to people around you. That's exactly how I felt—flawed.

So how did I cope? I built a defense. I found out it wasn't safe to be who I was, and so I worked very hard to find out who others wanted me to be. And then I did everything

I could to please them. I tried to perform as perfectly as possible in order to earn their approval because I had this crazy idea that if I earned enough of their approval, it would feel like love. Of course, it doesn't work that way. But I thought if I accumulated a lot of approval one day it would magically turn into love, which would satisfy those deep longings in my heart.

DEEP LONGINGS OF THE HEART

Let's stop for a moment and consider these deep longings of the heart. Maybe you're thinking, *I really don't want these deep longings. I'm angry that I have the desire to be loved. Life would be so much simpler if I just didn't feel that way.* But don't make the mistake of rejecting those deep longings that are normal in any love relationship. God gave you those desires of your heart in order to draw you to Him;

God gave you those desires of your heart in order to draw you to Him; we were created to be in an eternally secure love relationship with God.

we were created to be in an eternally secure love relationship with God. And that desire to belong is part of us, part of our soul as women, and not something to be despised. In fact, it is something we should respect; we should allow it to draw us closer to God.

When we're reeling from the painful sense that there's something wrong with us that I mentioned before, we begin to erect a defense system. I call it "defense by pretense." We pretend to be a perfect person, and criticism of any kind feels terribly threatening. The immediate response is, *Oh my goodness. They're not going to love me anymore. They're not going to approve of me anymore. They'll see me for the hopelessly flawed person I know I am.* And this kind of thinking reinforces unbiblical shame.

The problem with unbiblical shame is that it puts us in a state of fear. We fear we'll be abandoned because shame tells us something is terribly wrong with us. You see, when people face true moral guilt, they fear *punishment*. But when they deal with a false guilt or unbiblical shame, they fear *abandonment*.

And so we begin to build a defense system in order to

protect our wounded souls. It becomes a kind of defensive personality structure. We developed it so early in our lives, we aren't usually even aware of it. Actually, it can become the core of our identity. In effect, we become our defenses.

So how can you recognize if you've created a defensive personality structure? Though there are exceptions, of course, there are generalities that most people will relate to if they've struggled in this area of self-concept.

THE SEVEN AREAS OF A WOMAN'S LIFE

In order to recognize elements of a wounded soul, consider seven major areas of a woman's life.

1. *The Spiritual Area.* A woman who's created a defensive personality structure will possess a deep sense of being unlovable or too unforgivable for God. Therefore, she will feel alienated from her deity, convinced he is both disappointed and angry with her. But this concept of God is referred to as deity with a small "d." This is not God. This is not the God of the Bible. This is not the *Abba* whom Jesus called out to. This is a distorted deity that those of us who

struggle with unbiblical shame are hopelessly trying to please. And of course, you never can please this unloving concept you have imagined.

When such women become true Christian believers, a great deal of confusion takes place. We know that God's Word says He loves us. Yet when we struggle with this deep wound to our self-concept, we feel as if we're less worthy and therefore we can only claim a second-class kind of salvation. We're convinced that God doesn't really love us as much as He grudgingly tolerates us. After all, we reason, God made a deal with Jesus that if He would die on the cross to forgive our sins and if we would believe and ask Jesus into our hearts, then we would become a part of God's family forever. God wishes we weren't a part of the family, we think, but since He wants to be true to His Word He grudgingly accepts us as one of His children. That may sound ridiculous to some of you, but it's a thought process that many of us harbor deep in our hearts. I know because I've met numerous Christian women all over this country and in other places of the world who struggle with this in their spiritual lives.

2. *The Personal Area.* When we feel spiritually flawed, inadequate, and worthless, this perspective spills over into all facets of life. We feel inadequate no matter where we are. No matter what we do, it isn't good enough. We often have a sense of "outsiderliness"; we don't know how to connect, and we compensate for this by frantically pursuing perfectionism. We are literally driven to be perfect in everything. And that is a painful way to live.

3. *The Relational Area.* The third major area of a woman's life has to do with her relationships with others. With the defensive personality there is an insecurity about belonging. Understandably, this kind of woman has a strong need to earn acceptance and approval. She would no doubt feel unsafe if she received criticism from anyone important in her life. Those who struggle with this often have trouble relaxing when they're with others, because they work so hard to please everyone around them.

Women in general are often interested in pleasing people. We study people and determine exactly what they want from us, and then we try to fulfill their expectations as perfectly as possible. The sense of well-being in women,

Christian women in particular, fluctuates as the quality of our relationships fluctuate. If a conflict arises in one of our important relationships, we can't possibly feel all right about ourselves or about life. We are miserable. We may struggle with the fear of abandonment, rejection, criticism, and anger with anything that suggests the withdrawal of love or approval. With a defensive personality, the struggle is a hundred times worse.

4. *The Rational Area.* The fourth major area of a woman's life is the rational area, or the way we think. A woman grappling with a defensive personality has a preponderance of misbeliefs about God, about herself, and about others. If you were raised in a way that contributed to developing a distorted and faulty self-concept, then it's very likely that you developed a number of lies in your belief system. However, you didn't know they were lies because you believed what you were taught by your family. You had no way to discern the truth. Therefore, your belief system is as misshapen as your self-concept.

5. *The Emotional Area.* The next major element in the defensive personality structure is a woman's emotional life.

This is characterized by a great deal of sadness, possibly even depression, anxiety, and/or anger, which she uses to hide her fear of abandonment. Genesis 3 tells us that the first emotion mentioned after the Fall was fear. God knows we struggle with fear of abandonment. Consider how many "Fear not, for I am with yous" are in the Bible. God assures us He won't abandon us.

6. *The Volitional Area.* This element of the defensive personality structure deals with the choices and decisions women make. Typically, women in this situation make choices to gain and maintain acceptance. They operate by what I call the "automatic yes." Such women never think to check their schedule, check with their spouse, or pray before committing. Rather than possibly disappointing someone, they agree to everything. In effect, their decision becomes a defense tactic rather than a carefully considered response.

7. *The Behavioral Area.* This is the outward expression of a woman's life. If a woman has developed a defensive personality structure, she becomes overly focused on her relationships with others. In effect, relationships with other people take precedence over a relationship with God or healthy

maintenance of herself. Her entire sense of well-being becomes tied into her connection with others. And this attitude will be seen in her behavior.

It should now be obvious that a defensive personality structure presses an individual into a painful way of living. There's very little sense of fulfillment. In fact, most of the time we feel empty. It's as though we have holes in our soul— the truth of God's Word trickles out and doesn't seem to make a difference. And we are not deeply changed. Naturally, this is very confusing and very painful to Christian women.

DEVELOPING A SENSE OF FULFILLMENT

The question now becomes, What can we do about this? What must we do to experience a deep change and genuine fulfillment? How can we help others experience it? So far we've examined the defensive personality structure. Now I want us to consider the ideal structure. And as we do, we will discover how to experience deep healing and a true sense of fulfillment.

First of all, as we consider the ideal personality structure in a woman's life, I want to point out that I'll often use words like *more consistently* and *increasingly*. These are *process* words. Developing the ideal self-concept and personality structure is a process. It's not some magical step. It's a lifelong process of transformation.

First, let's consider the spiritual area. A woman in this situation will develop an increasingly deep sense of being fully known, fully loved, and freely forgiven by *Abba*, God. *Abba* is a word Jesus used, and the apostle Paul used that word in Romans and in Galatians. If translated, it would mean Daddy. It's an endearing word for father. A child would not call a male neighbor *Abba*. Therefore, part of the transformation in the spiritual life of a woman would be this deep sense that God is a loving daddy. He's not an angry, disappointed, scowling parent figure. He wants to love and protect us. As a result, we begin to function out of a sense of being cherished.

There's a huge difference between being forgiven and being cherished! God does not grudgingly accept us. He adores us. We are genuinely, truly, fully forgiven. It is such a profound change. Note what Paul says in Ephesians 2:13: "You who once were far away have been brought near." We've been transplanted.

Another important verse to consider is Ephesians 3:17, because it captures the key to this entire soul-healing process.

The deep change that occurs when we finally accept the freedom God's unconditional love affords us changes everything. It absolutely changes our entire lives!

"And I pray that Christ will be more and more at home in your hearts as you trust in him. May your roots go down deep into the soil of God's marvelous love" (NLT). But those of us with wounded self-concepts, with distorted and unbiblical self-concepts, have been rooted in painful soil. The deep change that occurs when we finally accept the freedom of God's unconditional love changes everything. It absolutely changes our entire lives!

But maybe you're thinking, *I know Scripture, I've read those passages before, and I go to a Bible-preaching church.* That is good. James 1:23–25 tells us that Scripture is a mirror and we can gain a much better view of who we are, who God is, and who others are from God's Word. Scripture study is so important. But knowing *about* God's love is not the same thing as experiencing the reality of it in your life. In John 17:3, Jesus tells us, "This is eternal life: that they may know you." Not that they may know *about* you. Anybody can know about God. In fact, pagans might even admit that God loves the world. There's a huge difference, though, between knowing God loves the world and experiencing the reality that He loves you. God loves you personally. It is literally life-transforming!

HEALING YOUR SOUL

If we want to experience a healing of our soul we must develop a *love* relationship with God. It has to be a relationship that goes beyond a theological certainty and becomes an experienced reality. I go into a lot of detail about this in my book *Into Abba's Arms,* and I offer numerous suggestions and examples of how to develop this relationship. Experiencing the reality that God loves *you* personally will have a profound healing effect on every area of your personality. I am learning this day by day.

Healing in the personal area of a woman's life would involve a secure sense of being unworthy but not worthless, with a consistent focus on God's adequacy rather than our own inadequacy. Notice the balance. Yes, we are unworthy of this eternal love relationship, but we are *not* worthless. The worth of something is determined by the price someone is willing to pay for it. Look at the price that was paid to allow us to enter into this eternally secure love relationship with God. How awesome! And as the roots of our life sink more and more deeply into the soil of God's marvelous love, we will experience what it is to live out of a sense of belovedness, a sense of secure belonging.

Healing in the relational area of a woman's life involves an increasingly secure sense of belonging, with a growing capacity to tolerate criticism. As our love relationship with God takes center stage in our life, we will be able to face this reality about relationships with others: *They all end.* All human relationships end. Even before they end, they fail to fully satisfy those deep longings of our soul. Ironically, we continue to expect them to satisfy us. And then we're disappointed. Following that, we become angry with the person who failed to meet our deep longings. Or we may be angry with God or ourselves, because we think it's all our fault. But it is foolish to expect human beings to supply what only God can.

In the Book of Jeremiah, God paints a vivid picture of His people and says they made two gigantic mistakes: "My people have committed two sins: They have forsaken me, the spring of living water, and have dug their own cisterns [wells], broken cisterns that cannot hold water" (Jeremiah 2:13 NLT). It's a metaphor for our soul-thirst. Rather than go to God, who is the only One who can satisfy with the Living Water, we forsake God and turn to broken cisterns—people or things—that cannot quench our relational thirst. The wonderful thing is, the more we sink our roots into the soil of God's marvelous love, the more we develop realistic expectations for our human relationships. It isn't that we don't value them. I cherish my husband and we've been married forty-five years. But I don't expect him to meet all my deepest relational longings, although he loves me very much.

Another marvelous benefit of turning to God first is we don't struggle nearly as much with a sense of loneliness, because we develop an abiding sense of God's presence with us at all times. He is as real to us as our children and husband. This may have always been a part of our theology, but now it becomes the foundation of our life.

In the rational area of a woman's life, there will be increased truthful reasoning because her mind is constantly being renewed. A scripture that fits perfectly here is Romans 12:2, where we're told to be transformed by the renewing of our mind. Yes, go deep into the Word. Find out more about who you are in Christ. Discover what healthy relationships with others are like. Learn more about the attributes of God. Read good Christian books. Seek out an older, wise, well-balanced Christian woman who can function as a mentor and discipler. And if you need to get some counseling, by all means, get counseling. I have done this myself, and it's been very helpful. There are numerous ways to correct our misbeliefs and develop more truthful ways of reasoning.

In the emotional area of a woman's life, most emotions will be expressed appropriately. Not perfectly. Will we sometimes express them inappropriately? Yes, because we're in process. But we will express them more and more appropriately as we develop. There will also be a substantial decrease in our fear of abandonment, since we will have an ever-increasing understanding that God is with us and will never abandon us.

In the volitional area of life—our choices—we will begin to make consistently responsible, biblically informed choices with an increased willingness to own them and their consequences. In other words, we won't look to blame others for our decisions. We will be comfortable taking responsibility for our choices.

We will not substitute an automatic "no" for an automatic "yes." Instead, we will begin to consider what God wants us to do. We will be less concerned about the approval of others and more concerned about the approval of God.

And then, finally, in our behavioral life, we will demonstrate increasingly mature, Christlike actions, characterized by genuine conviction and compassion. In other words, we will be more congruent. What we say and do will match who we are on the inside. This is an ongoing process, and it will grow stronger as we mature in our relationship with the Lord.

What a contrast! Everything will change in our lives when we begin to enter into the reality of this relationship with God, as the roots of life sink deeply into the soil of His marvelous love. But that makes sense when you stop to think about it. As we spend time with God, dialoguing with Him in prayer and reading His Word, we begin to change. And the way we view ourselves also begins to change. The reason this makes sense is that our self-concepts were formed originally within a relationship as we dialogued with a loved and trusted authority figure. And they will be TRANS-formed the same way.

Oh, what glorious change! Yes, there is a true hope for Christian women to have a satisfying self-concept, a secure identity, and genuine fulfillment.

Ephesians 3:17, 19-20 says, "I pray that Christ will be more and more at home in your hearts as you trust in him. May your roots go down deep into the soil of God's marvelous love. . . . May you experience the love of Christ, though it is so great you will never fully understand it. Then you will be filled with the fullness of life" (NLT). Literally, we will be fulfilled. Filled with the fullness of life and power that comes from God. Then Paul launches into praise for God: "Glory to God! By his mighty power at work within us, he is able to accomplish infinitely more than we would ever dare to ask or hope" (NLT).

I believe that as we increasingly experience God's "mighty power at work within us," we will understand that the issue is not our inadequacy. The real issue is *His* adequacy. And as we continue to draw closer to Christ, we will have an ever-deepening assurance that the answer to the question of our identity is this: I am the beloved child of my *Abba* God.

ABOUT THE AUTHOR

Sandra D. Wilson is a retired family therapist, a counseling consultant, seminary professor, internationally sought-after speaker, and best-selling author of six books. Sandra holds the following degrees: a B.S. from the University of Cincinnati, an M.A. from the University of Louisville, and a Ph.D. from the Union Institute.

Verses That Inspire

"I know the plans I have for you," declares the LORD, "plans to prosper you and not to harm you, plans to give you hope and a future." (Jeremiah 29:11)

You are no longer foreigners and aliens, but fellow citizens with God's people and members of God's household. (Ephesians 2:19)

"The LORD your God is with you, he is mighty to save. He will take great delight in you; he will quiet you with his love, he will rejoice over you with singing." (Zephaniah 3:17)

Who shall separate us from the love of Christ? . . . For I am convinced that neither death nor life, neither angels nor demons, neither the present nor the future, . . . nor anything else in all creation, will be able to separate us from the love of God that is in Christ Jesus our Lord. (Romans 8:35, 38–39)

. . . The mind controlled by the Spirit is life and peace. (Romans 8:6)

. . . Those who are led by the Spirit are sons of God. For you did not receive a spirit that makes you a slave again to fear, but you received the Spirit of sonship. And by him we cry, "*Abba,* Father." The Spirit himself testifies with our spirit that we are God's children. (Romans 8:14-16)

Being a Godly Woman through Every Stage of Life

KATHLEEN HART

In all things God works for the good of those who love him,
who have been called according to his purpose.

—ROMANS 8:28

Life unfolds in stages. Thousands of years ago, King Solomon acknowledged that fact when he wrote in Ecclesiastes, "There is a time for everything, and a season for every activity under heaven" (3:1). Our lives consist of a wide variety of activities strewn through definite stages. Each stage is unique. Each stage contains a purpose—a calling from God.

As we travel through each of those phases, we need to keep our focus on God, who orchestrates every day of every stage of our lives.

Every woman faces many stages in her lifetime, particularly if she's a married woman with children. The stages of a woman's life include premarriage, marriage, newlywed, pregnancy, birth, parenting, career, homemaking, teenagers, caring for aging parents, and somewhere in-between, a midlife crisis. You may experience one, two, or more of these stages simultaneously, in varying order, or even skip over some.

Typically during the period of time that you have teens at home, you may also be caring for aging parents and dealing with a midlife crisis. Perhaps you're also facing a career change at this time. All of this happens during the midstages of a woman's life. At the same time you have to put extra effort into your marriage. Marriage can be hard work at any stage, and raising children is certainly always a challenge.

Once the kids are gone a woman enters the next stage—the empty nest syndrome. And as the children grow older, you may face some additional stages: the mother-in-law stage, the grandmother stage, the stage of menopause, and retirement. If you're fortunate you'll enjoy your golden years, and then there's death. What a wonderful stage eternity will be with Jesus! Of course, death may occur at any one of these stages—it might not happen at the end of a long life.

During these stages you may experience good times or bad, laughter or tears, poverty or wealth, sickness or health. Each stage brings different experiences and different challenges. The question is, How do we deal with those new challenges? Do we grow or diminish? I believe challenges can be confronted and turned to constructive use, or what I call "intentioned fulfillment in Christ."

In order to understand these stages we have to first be aware of them. Then we need to try to prepare ourselves for the next stage. We need to be flexible and adjust to the demands that each stage brings. "Adjust" is an important concept to apply to one's life in order to successfully move from one stage to the next. Otherwise, problems arise. Remember, the circumstances and experiences will be different for each woman. Each stage of life will not necessarily resemble that of another woman's because our children, husbands, and circumstances are different.

As you face the challenges of each stage of your life, there are six questions to ask yourself that will really help you cope.

1. Am I experiencing God's love at this stage of life?
2. How am I loving God?
3. What is my purpose for living?
4. Who is in my grandstand?
5. Am I in control of my actions and attitudes?
6. What lasting impression am I leaving?

Let's consider each of these questions in more depth.

1. AM I EXPERIENCING GOD'S LOVE AT THIS STAGE OF LIFE?

If I asked you, "Are you experiencing God's love now?" you might say, "Why ask that question? I know God loves me." Unfortunately, during difficult times in life when we're dealing with depression, failure, regrets, low self-esteem, anger, and hurt, we start blaming God. In fact, we wonder if He really loves us. We have all been through that stage where we feel, *Oh, I've been a failure. Look what I've done!* We grapple with regrets and think, *I wonder if God is disappointed with me. Does He really love me?* The simple answer is, Yes, God loves us—here, now, and just as we are. If we're dealing with a really stressful period, such as a physical illness or a debilitating challenge, it may be helpful to seek guidance from a doctor or a wise Christian counselor. This is important to remember. There are times when we cannot make it on our own and may need help. So if you feel beaten by a current situation in your life and you feel alienated from God and cannot cope, seek temporary professional help.

In A. W. Tozer's book *The Pursuit of God,* he says, "Wherever we are, God is here." Those words have been such an encouragement to me, especially when I travel to different parts of the world. In Hebrews 13:5, God says, "Never will I leave you; never will I forsake you." God is with us wherever we go. He's here with us at this very moment. When we come face to face with God, we must see ourselves as God sees us. The first thing to do, then, is to understand God's grace and love for us. Consider the words of Ephesians 3:18–19: "To grasp how wide and long and high and deep is the love of Christ [for me!], and to know this love that surpasses knowledge." And 1 John 4:19 tells us, "We love

In certain stages of life, we need to be reminded that nothing can separate us from the love of God.

[him] because he first loved us." Or look at Romans 5:8: "While we were still sinners, Christ died for us." And He loved us long before we loved Him. God loved us so much

He allowed His Son, Jesus, to die for us. In certain stages of life, we need to be reminded that nothing can separate us from the love of God.

Romans 8:38 tells us, "I am convinced that [nothing] . . . can separate us from the love of God that is in Christ Jesus our Lord." This offers us so much security, confidence, and a true sense of identity because each of us is a child of God. At certain points in our life we're really going to need to be reminded of God's unchanging, unfailing love.

Once we become convinced of His love, we must be willing to receive it. Our mind may acknowledge, *Yes, God loves me,* but we don't receive it; we don't truly allow God to love us. Romans 5:5 says, "God has poured out his love into our hearts by the Holy Spirit, whom he has given us." Our response should be, "I receive Your love, Lord."

I teach my students to breathe in and receive His love. I say, "I breathe in Your love, Lord, and I breathe out all negativity and unbelief." Once you have received His love and it is living within you, you will be able to love others with the overflow of His abundant love, which is poured in and through your heart. It's easy to pass on love when it has been given to you so generously.

2. HOW AM I LOVING GOD?

This question forces us to come face to face with ourselves. We must see ourselves as God sees us. In Psalm 139 God states that He knows us and is familiar with all our ways. God knows us just as we are, warts and all. Sometimes when we battle with low self-esteem or failure, we want to run away from God because we feel, *I've disappointed Him; He couldn't possibly love me.* But remember He loves us and died for us while we were yet sinners, and He'll never leave us. Psalm 44:21 tells us, "God . . . knows the secrets of the heart." He knows our every thought. We can't hide them from Him. In Psalm 139:24 we read, "See if there is any offensive way in me." And when we go to the Lord in prayer we need to ask, "Is there any offensive way in me, Lord? Is there something You need to show me that needs to be changed or removed at this stage of my life? Am I reacting to a situation incorrectly or even sinfully?"

This leads to the question, What or who do we love most in this world? God has created us, He's given us a magnificent home on earth, He sent His Son to die for our sins, and He also sent us the Holy Spirit to guide us through life. And in return for all this God asks us to love Him with all our heart, soul, strength, and mind. Jesus repeats almost the same words in Luke 10:27–28: "Love [me] with all your heart and with all your soul and with all your strength and with all your mind. . . . Do this and you will live." Do you want to live life to the fullest? Love God with all your heart, soul, strength, and mind. When we love God in this manner, He becomes our foundation and we become one with Jesus. Jesus expressed His desire to be one with us in John 17:21–22. He prayed, "[Father,] may they also be in us . . . that they may be one as we are one." In John 14:20, Jesus said, "I am in my Father, and you are in me, and I am in you." We are one. If we are one with Jesus, whatever happens to us, happens to Him. So we don't have to say, "Oh, Lord, look at what's happening." He already knows.

Strive to focus on Jesus, rather than on people or circumstances. As we focus on Jesus, it's very important to pray. In Philippians 4:6 we're told not to worry about anything, but instead, to pray about everything and tell God our needs. So pray about everything.

I really admire King David; he was so human, and he expressed himself honestly in the Psalms. In Psalm 142:1–2, David says, "I cry aloud to the LORD; I lift up my voice to the LORD for mercy. I pour out my complaint before him; before him I tell him my trouble." This is what we have to do. We pour out our heart to the Lord and share everything with Him. Pray about everything, everywhere, and at any time.

As a chaplain to students at Fuller Theological Seminary, I help prepare women to go into ministry, as well as encourage them in their personal and spiritual development. And I have taught them to carry prayer clocks. Each woman has her own prayer clock. I have one in my purse and it goes off at noon every day. All of us have made a pact to pray for each other at noon every day, so no matter where I am, no matter what part of the world, my clock goes off at noon California time and I pray. (Unfortunately, it goes off during the night when we're overseas sometimes, and my husband isn't very happy about that.)

I like what O. Hallesby says: "The spirit of prayer makes us so intimate with God that we scarcely pass through an experience before we speak to Him about it. Go to Him in supplication, in intercession, in fervent requests of thanksgiving and adoration." This is what prayer is all about. It's telling God everything at any time and any place.

3. WHAT IS MY PURPOSE FOR LIVING?

Have you ever felt overwhelmed or out of control? Maybe you've taken a wrong turn in your life. I know about wrong turns. When we first came to the United States, I studied electroencephalography and wasted four years of my life running ahead of the Lord with my own idea. It wasn't what He wanted for me, and I never used it. I went right up to becoming licensed. I had simply taken the wrong direction. So ask yourself, "What is my purpose for living?" The answer lies in 1 Corinthians 10:31, which says, "Whatever you do, do it all for the glory of God." I asked God to help me with this career, but I wasn't seeking His will or looking to glorify Him in the process. I was struggling through a midlife crisis at the time. It can be a very restless stage, forcing us to run in the wrong direction if we don't ask God for guidance. A stage in which to be cautious and alert.

Of course there are certain stages where life seems insane. And those of us who've parented teenagers know what that means. We become overloaded. We're running kids everywhere and wearing all different kinds of hats, and life just seems insane. I often refer to a line from Oswald Chambers in his book *My Utmost for His Highest*. He says, "We gain and maintain a strong, calm sanity." When my husband and I are in certain situations, especially at an airport, and everything's going wrong, I say to him, "Let's remember to have a strong, calm sanity." Of course, our strong, calm sanity comes from

the peace of knowing and loving the Lord and being confi-
dent of His presence and help.

Sometimes women experience a stage when they feel
restless and overloaded, and they lose their sense of identity.
This often happens when their children leave home. For
years we see ourself as a mother, and lots of love comes to us
at that stage. But when our children leave home, we lose this
identity. The same thing happens to men at retirement. And
then we feel unfulfilled. There's no joy in our life. In fact, we
can feel rather miserable and depressed. We ask ourselves,
"What is my purpose for living at this stage of my life?" But
the question you really need to ask is, "What does God want
me to accomplish at this time?"

It is important to focus on what we need to accomplish
right now, because sometimes we want to do things that are
not possible to accomplish at that particular stage of life. For
example, consider a mother with three young children who
has some great ideas for a career or an entrepreneurial enter-
prise. In reality it will be very difficult for her to accomplish
such an ambitious undertaking at this time. And it's no good
feeling like a failure or being frustrated, because we tend to

take out our frustration on our children and spouse. So we must regularly turn to God and ask, "What do You want to accomplish at this stage of my life?"

While we're anticipating God's answer to that question there are only two things to do: wait and listen. Psalm 130:5–6 says, "I wait for the LORD, my soul waits, and in his word I put my hope. My soul waits for the Lord . . ." It's so important to wait for the Lord, because it's very easy to run ahead of Him or become discontented. So we must wait on the Lord.

Be sure to listen. I only learned to listen much later in life, which I'm very sorry about, because it took me a long time to learn to listen to the Lord. It takes awhile to become attuned to His voice guiding you. Sometimes you'll go through phases when you might be completely unaware of Him. Life crowds in on you. But in order to hear God speak, you have to spend time in His Word because most of the time you will hear Him speak through Scripture. Whenever I talk at conferences, I explain to my audience that I have become a one-sentence listener and I'm amazed at what I have heard God say to me. I realized before this that I missed a lot of what He wanted to say to me. He even speaks through the most unlikely people at times. So listen to God. Be alert and wait on Him for direction.

This, then, naturally leads to finding one's direction in life. To do this correctly, we need to look to God to show us the way. Proverbs 3:5 says, "Trust in the LORD with all your heart . . ." If you love the Lord with all your heart, it's only natural to trust Him with all your heart. ". . . And lean not on your own understanding; in all your ways acknowledge him, and he will make your paths straight." He will point to the path you should take. We must trust Him for guidance when we seek His will. God has a plan for each one of us. Jeremiah 29:11 tells us, "I know the plans I have for you, . . . plans to prosper you and not to harm you, plans to give you hope and a future." Keep in mind, even if your career is on hold, your life is not. The Lord will show you the way as you trust Him with all your heart.

Here are some important points to keep in mind when looking for direction. The first one is to adjust to change. This is extremely important as we ease from one stage to the next. There are certain stages in life when *you* will have to change certain things about yourself, especially when you become a parent, because now your life is on display before your children. So be flexible and open to change. Flexibility is essential in life because if you're not flexible, you're going to break.

Sometimes in life we will experience what I call "the suddenlys." Suddenly the car develops a problem. Suddenly the washing machine breaks down. Suddenly there's an accident. Or you've planned a well-organized day, and suddenly something happens to alter your plans. Those are "the suddenlys." Be flexible or you'll have trouble coping. But in spite of these temporary though annoying challenges, remain faithful to the Lord. Just tell yourself, "This too shall pass."

It's also important, as you seek direction in your life during various stages, that you grieve the losses that cannot be changed. There are some tough situations in life that cannot be changed. I have shared with women how to grieve over these life situations—then get on with life. We must allow ourselves time to feel our grief, otherwise depression and unhappiness will settle over us that can remain for the rest of our lives.

Next, we must understand our priorities. Somebody sent me a book at Christmas called *A Mother's Journey*. Some of the words in the book really touched me.

God as the Shepherd says,
Give me your hopes, give me your dreams,
    the journey is long and not what it seems.
Affirm children, be faithful to Me,
    this is the mother I want you to be.

I like those words, "be faithful to Me." That's what the Lord wants us to do in every stage of life—be faithful to Him. Not successful or wealthy or superintelligent, just faithful. The Book of Revelation talks a lot about being faithful and receiving a crown for our faithfulness.

As we journey through each stage of life, we need to also develop what I call "a satisfied heart." Normally, human beings are not satisfied. We are far more easily dissatisfied. So learn how to develop a satisfied heart and life will become a peaceful adventure rather than a disappointment. Grasp the moments. So many young mothers say, "What am I doing with my life? It feels like such a waste!" Grasp the moments. You're only going to have those children for a little while and then they're going to grow up into teenagers and before you know it, they are adults. Some of those moments will be "one-and-only" moments, such as a wonderful day at the beach with the children when we think, *Oh, I wish we could be like this all the time.* Or you and your husband enjoy a peaceful time in your marriage and you think, *Let's stay like this for-ever.* In Anne Morrow Lindbergh's book *A Gift from the Sea,* she talks about "one-and-only" moments in life. These are treasured, memorable moments, but unfortunately we can-not remain in these moments. Choose to be satisfied with Jesus and have His peace in this moment.

4. Who Is in My Grandstand?

This question has helped me so much in life. My husband thought this one up and uses it in conferences when he's addressing pastors and their wives. He explains that all of us play to a specific audience. For some it might be our par-ents; for others it might be our spouse or other people. It's important to recognize whose approval controls your life. Whose approval are you living for and organizing your life for, in order to please them? Is it yourself? Others? God? Second Corinthians 5:9 says, "We make it our goal to please the Lord." Our goal should be to please the Lord. Clear your grandstand of all other people. The only one who should be there is Jesus. He's the one who loves you unconditionally. He's the one you should love with all your heart. He's the one giving you direction in your life. At each stage of your life, ask again, "Who is in my grandstand? Who am I trying to please?" Believe me, you'll never be able to please everybody. So make Jesus the Lord of your life and let Him be the only One in your grandstand.

5. AM I IN CONTROL OF MY ACTIONS AND ATTITUDES?

Do you choose to act, or do you react to your circumstances? This principle has made a big difference in my life, because it has set me free in all my relationships—in my marriage, with my children, and in my ministry. Human nature is such that we are perpetually *reacting* to others. Take, for example, two children who are playing with one another. One sticks his finger in the other's eye, and then the other one sticks his finger in the first one's eye. And before you know it, they're slapping each other. They're reacting to what each did. Unfortunately, many children become adults and still act like this. They remain reactors.

So how do we avoid being perpetual negative reactors? First, take control of your actions and attitudes by preparing yourself ahead of time. If you give some thought to how you act in a given situation, you will not be as likely to react.

God's Word clearly points out how we should and should not act. Romans 12:14–21 tells us not to curse, not to be proud, not to be conceited, not to repay evil for evil, not to take revenge, not to be overcome by evil but to overcome evil with good. And Luke 6:37 says not to judge or condemn. How should we act? We are told in Luke 6:27 to do good, bless, pray for, love, and forgive our enemies. There it is. That is how we should act toward others. It doesn't mean we're never going to react negatively. But if we are prepared, we'll be able to deal with it. So take control of your actions and attitudes.

The next thing to tackle is to stop blaming other people and circumstances for your negative behavior. People love to blame their parents or spouse or other people because they've become angry or because of negative behavior. This must be stopped. Take responsibility for who you are, for your behavior, and for your actions and attitudes. We have to do that at every stage of our life. Otherwise, we'll continue to react to life, to circumstances, and to people, and our life will become miserable.

We need to take control of our thoughts. We can either be our greatest encourager or our greatest discourager. We have to take control of what we think. Take stock of your self-talk. Do you put yourself down or do you tell yourself you're the best? We often talk about time management, but thought management will make a big difference in our lives.

Always encourage yourself in the Lord. I remember during my midlife crisis stage, I was always trying to run away from myself. I turned to other people for encouragement, such as my husband or my friends. Since then, I've learned to be my own best encourager. I've put together a photo album that contains verses that encourage me, challenge me, guide me. I refer to these often. I've passed these verses on to my students' wives. Encourage yourself in the Lord as David did in a stressful time. First Samuel 30:6 says, "David was greatly distressed. . . . But David found strength in the LORD his God." He turned to the Lord and leaned on Him in times of trouble. We all need to do that. In Jude 1:20 we are told, "Build yourself up in your most holy faith and pray in the Holy Spirit."

It is important to memorize Scripture. In my house, I have laminated cards posted in the bathroom, kitchen, and bedroom. This helps me memorize the verses. I also have some laminated cards on my treadmill. In fact, I'm known as the lady who laminates with love, and I've sent my cards all over the world. I've shared them with others because the verses have helped me so much. In fact, a pastor's wife passed one of my cards to President Bush, and he carries it in his pocket. He said, "This will always be with me."

In addition to my cards, I also have framed verses in my house. I've purchased some attractive frames and placed these verses in various rooms of my house, and these, too, build me up in the Lord. So you see, I don't depend on other people to keep my spirits up. During various stages of life, we will be faced with loneliness and heartache, and we have to learn to prepare ourselves beforehand. In this way, when difficulty arises, we are strong in the Lord, faithful to Him, and we don't have to depend on others for encouragement.

You must always focus on the responsibilities in your life at the present moment. Once those are realized and accepted, you will be able to avoid a lot of struggles and dissatisfaction, frustration and loneliness. Focusing on your current responsibilities also prevents you from neglecting the people and things that fall under your care. I teach a class of young mothers whose husbands are entering the ministry or preparing to be counselors or psychologists or missionaries. And facing this issue is very important for them because their careers are currently on hold. But I always remind them, "Your life is not on hold. God has a plan for you right now."

6. WHAT LASTING IMPRESSION AM I LEAVING?

The sixth question to ask yourself in each stage of your life is this: "What lasting impression am I leaving?" Edmond

Haraucourt said, "We leave behind a bit of ourselves wherever we have been." And this is true. Wherever you go, whether it's the home, the grocery store, the office, or the bank, you're leaving a bit of yourself behind. The question is, How are we affecting other people's lives as we're going through these stages of life? How do people feel about themselves after they have been with us? Do they feel encouraged? Are we conducting ourselves in a winsome way, a way that will lead others to Christ?

Keep in mind, our children incorporate our attitudes, actions, and words into their approach to life. Remember you're role modeling for your children as you go through these various stages. And when you're traveling through the years, your children are really watching how you conduct yourself. Maybe you're caring for aged parents at this time and struggling through a midlife crisis. You are making a deep impression on those teenagers. So it's important that you take control, find your direction, and be aware of the impression you're leaving on your children. In fact, prepare yourself beforehand for those teenage years by reading books, watching videos, and talking to parents who have come through that time. The way you raise your children may be the way they will eventually raise their own children, good or bad.

So the way we live each stage of our life leaves a lasting impression on others and a legacy. Second Corinthians 2:15 talks about a fragrance; we are the fragrance of Christ. Our love is like an open book, and hopefully the people around us are reading it. Second Corinthians 3:18 tells us we are being transformed into the likeness of Christ.

> *The way we live each stage of our life leaves a lasting impression on others and a legacy.*

When this concept of leaving a lasting impression on my children and grandchildren really occurred to me, I decided to write a booklet, which I called *Words of Life and Words from Nana,* for each of them with his or her name on it. It includes my testimony and a personal letter written to each one. There are also verses of encouragement in the booklets, as well as one particular incident relating to the child's life and why he or she is so special to me. My husband built a beautiful box for each grandchild as well. It was the child's treasure box, with a specially made gold plate on the top engraved with his or her name, the date, and the words "from Papa." I wish my grandparents or parents had given me such a booklet and box. I would treasure them, and I could pass them on to my grandchildren. I'm hoping my grandkids will want to pass my booklet on to their children. You see, I don't want my life lived simply in words. I've tried to live my life in a Christlike manner. I hope my grandchildren see glimpses of the Lord in me. This, I believe, is what it means to leave a lasting impression: that your life reflects your love of the Lord and that future generations will follow in your footsteps, seeking to glorify our heavenly Father.

I pray that you will be blessed in each stage of your life. Remember, God is with you. He is there, at every stage of your life. He is there to uphold you, and with the help of the Lord you can be an extraordinary woman of God throughout your life. May you always love Him with all your heart and be faithful to Him. God bless you.

ABOUT THE AUTHOR

Kathleen Hart is chaplain to student wives at Fuller Theological Seminary, where she leads weekly classes and provides individual counseling. She is also a popular speaker at seminars and conferences for women. She and her husband, Archibald Hart, minister worldwide to pastors and their spouses. They also present marriage enrichment seminars.

VERSES THAT INSPIRE

I can do everything through him who gives me strength. (Philippians 4:13)

We are not trying to please men but God, who tests our hearts. (1 Thessalonians 2:4)

We have confidence before God and receive from him anything we ask, because we obey his commands and do what pleases him. (1 John 3:21-22)

I urge you . . . to offer your bodies as living sacrifices, holy and pleasing to God—this is your spiritual act of worship. Do not conform any longer to the pattern of this world, but be transformed by the renewing of your mind. Then you will be able to test and approve what God's will is—his good, pleasing and perfect will. (Romans 12:1–2)

Rejoice in the Lord always. I will say it again: Rejoice! Let your gentleness be evident to all. The Lord is near. Do not be anxious about anything, but in everything, by prayer and petition, with thanksgiving, present your requests to God. (Philippians 4:4–6)

As Jesus Cared for Women

DAVID HAGER, M.D.

Everyone should be quick to listen, slow to speak
and slow to become angry.

—JAMES 1:19

As a medical doctor, I see a wide variety of female patients who come into my office with many different problems. I've discovered something about these women: The one thing they all have in common is that they want to be heard. Listening is one of the key aspects of being a physician since we make most of our diagnoses by listening to complaints, not through technology. It is so important for a woman to feel she has someone's undivided attention—someone who will *really* listen.

My patients have suffered through a number of different problems, such as abuse, severe anxiety and depression, menstrual disorders or problems related to reproduction, addictions, fatigue, and overwhelming discouragement. A common thread that connects many of these situations is these women have never truly been heard. They make an appointment to address their medical problems, but they also come to be counseled, to have someone listen to them. Women want to be heard, women want to be taken seriously, and women want to know how God can help them.

Several years ago as I searched for ways to counsel these women, I asked God to give me direction. One night, as I was praying, God said to me, "Have you ever thought of looking at My Word? To find out how women should be treated, look at Jesus' interactions with women." It only takes a quick study of Scripture to discover that Jesus broke all the cultural codes of His time in terms of His treatment toward women. He extended dignity and respect toward them, something that had never before been seen in that culture. So when people say that the Bible espouses a patriarchal system, they are ignoring this evidence. Jesus honored women, and since Jesus was part of the Godhead—Father, Son, and Holy Spirit—the respect He had for women was conveyed to Him from God.

The Master Gardener

I'm a gardener. I do all of our landscaping at home. I love to watch things grow. So when I read the Bible I'm naturally drawn to the analogy of Jesus as the Master Gardener. And I think there are several examples of Jesus' interactions with us in which He exemplifies that role.

First, He selects the land. Before a gardener ever begins to plant, he or she must select a specific location. In Jesus' case, He selected you. He's called you to be one of His own— to be intimately related to Him.

Second, a gardener prepares the soil. Seeds and bulbs are never planted unless the soil has been tilled and the rocks and the weeds removed. This can be a painful process. When

God pulls the weeds from my heart and life, when He starts removing rocks, it hurts. But preparation of the soil is critically important so the seed that is sown will have a chance to grow.

Next comes the planting. He plants His Word in our life just like a gardener lovingly plants seeds. He relates to you through His Word and through prayer, which develops an intimate relationship, a one-on-one relationship that Jesus wants to have with us. Is your soil rocky or fertile? Has it been adequately prepared?

The fourth thing God does is He waters and waits. He wants to irrigate your life. Some gardeners plant a garden, but they skimp on water. That doesn't work. You have to provide adequate water as well as fertilizer. And then you must be patient. But we are not always patient; we want to do things in our own time. We don't want to wait on God's timing. More often then not, His timing is much different than ours, but we have to remind ourselves that His timing is perfect.

Finally, when all the preparation is complete, a bountiful harvest can be enjoyed. This is a time for rejoicing! Jesus wants to be the gardener of your life. First Peter 5:6 tells us,

"Humble yourselves, therefore, under God's mighty hand that he may lift you up in due time. Cast all your anxiety on him because he cares for you." Yes, our heavenly Father and Jesus care for you.

Lessons from Jesus' Ministry

There are several examples of Jesus interacting with women during His ministry years. All of them are worth studying in more depth because there's a valuable lesson to be learned in each one.

The first lesson deals with respect. Luke 7:36–38 records the story of the woman who entered Simon's house for a celebration. Jesus attends the party, along with His friends and probably some of His disciples. They are enjoying themselves when this woman wanders in off the street and suddenly falls at the feet of Jesus. Overcome with emotion, her tears fall upon Jesus' legs and feet, and she uses her long hair to wipe His feet clean. In this example we not only see a woman with a contrite heart who's seeking forgiveness, but also a woman who demonstrates an enormous amount of love and devotion. Now imagine yourself to be a typical religious leader. Don't you think you might have been a little indignant if a prostitute had approached you in such a matter? But Jesus had the greatest respect for this woman and He understood that this was an eternally significant moment. He knew she had probably been shamed and blamed all her life, but Jesus received her and accepted her, then He rebuked the religious leaders for their lack of manners. They hadn't anointed His head with oil or washed His feet as this woman had done. What a wonderful example of Jesus demonstrating His respect for another person. Do you know that Jesus also respects you? In fact, Jesus feels this way about you regardless of your past.

The second lesson is one of love. Mark 5:35–43 reveals one of the greatest examples of Jesus' love when Jesus healed Jairus's daughter. But just before this occurred, Jesus was walking through a large crowd when someone touched the hem of His tunic.

"Someone touched Me," Jesus told Peter (see Luke 8:43–48). Peter probably burst out laughing and said, "Sure somebody touched You. We're surrounded by a huge crowd."

"No," Jesus said. "Somebody touched Me because I felt

healing power go out of My body" (my paraphrase). Jesus recognized that someone who was suffering needed Him. And how did He react? Was He indignant? Did He ignore the situation by saying, "I've got other business to attend to. I must heal a little girl, who may be dead by now"? No, He stopped and asked the woman to identify herself out of the crowd. He didn't want to shame or blame her. He treated her with love. Bleeding for years and poverty-stricken because she had been to so many doctors who were unable to help her, she was desperate for a cure.

Jesus is more than ready to forgive each one of us.

There's great significance to this story for two reasons. First, this woman would have never been out in public. When a Jewish woman bled, she could not be seen in public for fear that she would contaminate others. Second, she would have never touched a rabbi while she was bleeding because that would have contaminated his sacred call—to intercede for the people to seek atonement for their sins. This woman really risked her reputation, her position in the community, her church membership—risked everything—but

Jesus understood. He asked her to identify herself, and when she did, He lovingly assured her that He recognized her faith and she had been healed. Her bleeding stopped, and she went home healed and forgiven.

The third lesson concerns forgiveness. Jesus is more than ready to forgive each one of us. A good example of this is in John 8:2–11, where a woman is "caught" in the act of adultery. This means she was actually found in bed with a man and brought before the religious leaders to be stoned to death. And what was Jesus' response when they asked Him, "What should we do with this woman?" He knelt down and wrote something in the sand, but no one knows what it was. He allowed time for the accusers to consider their statements of accusation.

The puzzling piece of this adultery case concerns the man who was caught in adultery. Why was he not charged? A double standard existed then and still exists today. We tend to be much more critical of a woman involved in an extra-marital relationship than we are of a man. For some reason, society seems to think it's more acceptable for a man to be unfaithful than a woman. But Jesus didn't see it that way. He recognized their sin of judgment as well as her sexual sin. Jesus always looks straight at the heart. He knew this woman had made mistakes, had committed a sin, but she wanted to be forgiven. So He said, "Let those who have never sinned throw the first stones" (John 8:7 NLT). They all disappeared rather quickly after that, the oldest first because they had more sin to confess. Then Jesus turned back to the woman, who now stood alone, and said, "Go and sin no more" (NLT).

The next lesson focuses on communication. John 4:5–42 contains my favorite story—the woman at the well. Here was a woman with a sordid past who had come to collect water from the well. The interesting thing about this story is that Jesus didn't *have* to travel through Samaria, a land despised by the Jews, but He did. His detour brought him to Jacob's well, and now the disciples were tired and hungry, so they hurried off to search for food and water. A woman approached the well where Jesus had stayed behind, and He asked her for a drink of water. She's flabbergasted that a man would speak to her, especially since He's Jewish; and she's surprised, too, that He would ask her for a favor. But on this day Jesus had a date with destiny. Meeting this woman was critically important, because her individual sin and need for forgiveness were only part of the whole picture. There was an entire community in need of forgiveness and Jesus knew that this woman was about to become an evangelist to the people. So what did He do? He communicated the truth to her.

Communication—it's what women crave the most but receive the least from their mates. It is the beginning of intimacy. Unfortunately, most men believe sex is the beginning of intimacy. Intimacy, however, begins with interaction, with communication. What could possibly express commitment, concern, and genuine love more than a person who is willing to listen? And what exactly is required to be a good listener? We have to focus all our attention on the other person. To listen well, we have to be willing to set aside our own interests, which requires a degree of humility that isn't possible for me without a lot of prayer and a lot of help from the Holy Spirit. When I don't take the time to listen, what am I communicating to my spouse? I'm communicating withdrawal, detachment, disinterest, disrespect, and hostility. None of these reflects love. As we consider how Jesus cared for women, we know that one of the primary ways was by listening, talking to, and interacting with them. His actions and words always revealed this statement: "You matter to Me; you're important to Me."

In marriage, couples develop a rhythm of coming together and then pulling away that might be called the "on-off switch" of relationships. Don't be fooled into thinking that sex is the "on-off switch." Rather, good sex is what a couple enjoys after they've established communication. It's a delight of the senses after they've connected with their minds and hearts. Unfortunately, our culture strongly favors individualism, and it permeates everything in our "me-first" society. People remain with a loved one until their interest wanes, then they move on to someone else who more fully captures their attention.

Many years ago on a television program a couple was married and their vows were considered quite radical. Instead of saying, "Till death do us part," they said, "Till love do us part." But Christians seek to make a deeper commitment. And when we listen to our mates and when our mates are willing to listen to us, we are communicating that our commitment will last beyond the feel-good stages, that it will last as long as life shall last. We are committing ourselves for a lifetime. Biblical cultures valued attachment. In fact, the Bible tells us, "A man will leave his father and mother and be united to his wife" (Ephesians 5:31). First Corinthians 7:10 and 7:39 tell us that we are to remain with our spouse for a lifetime. That's the kind of commitment necessary in a marriage; it's intended to last until death separates the couple (Matthew 19:4–6).

Look at it this way: Listening to your spouse in a totally focused manner is like giving him or her a gift—a gift of loving attention. Let's be a little more specific now and consider how a wife can engage in listening skills that say, "I care about you," to her husband. Even though our topic focuses on Jesus and women, I believe Jesus cared for women the same way He cared for all people—with a compassionate, loving heart. So let's consider some of the listening skills we might do well to learn to enhance our relationships.

Listening requires a great deal of humility, because saying less when you could have said more allows God to do everything. Someone once described a Christian servant as one who is willing to do less so that God can do more. Isn't that a wonderful concept of servanthood? But in order for the Holy Spirit to do His work, we must accept a humble position. And never is that more appropriate than in listening to your spouse.

The first thing we need to do is to prepare to listen, which requires being still. What does Scripture say? "Be still, and know that I am God" (Psalm 46:10). Focusing on that other person communicates, "I care for you." Then we need to develop eye contact, although sometimes it's hard to look into each other's eyes because we may feel anger or guilt. After connecting eye to eye, confess your wrongs and then open your heart and mind to listen. Let your partner talk. Even if your spouse doesn't seem to make sense, let him talk. Be willing to listen to your husband in silence, be quiet as he shares his feelings, and by so doing you'll communicate, "You are important to me."

Once you've listened carefully and your partner is ready for you to talk, it's important to communicate with "I" messages, such as, "When you say this, I feel that." Or, "I think I hear you saying that you're upset about the children." Simply repeat back to your partner what you've heard him or her say to be sure that you understand the issue. Then when you've listened and talked, pray together. Come to some kind of agreement in the presence of the Holy Spirit. Search God's Word for His advice on the issue at hand. Maybe you will agree to set aside the issue and talk about it later. Perhaps you will agree to hold separate opinions, but you'll agree not to fight about it anymore. There is no set rule about settling differences. But the most loving gift one partner can give to the other partner is undivided attention. Jesus' example of this as seen in John 4:1–42 with the woman at the well should inspire us all.

In our day and age, the Samaritan woman might have been someone we would condemn. Maybe we would point out the error of her ways rather than reach out to her in love. But what did Jesus do? He loved her enough to talk to her— and then listen. He acknowledged her as a person. Then, and only then, did He begin to instruct her. We're the same way. When we feel listened to, when we feel we've really been heard, we are much more teachable; we're more willing to listen to a correction or a suggestion that our partner passes on to us.

Jesus knew how to communicate with the Samaritan woman. He broke down the barriers between them and found out who she was. In fact, He even began to tell her things about herself that only she knew. Immensely impressed, she ran back to her village. She told the townspeople that Jesus must be the Messiah, and she eventually led the entire community back to the well. The biblical accounts tell us that Jesus and His disciples stayed two more days and brought many townspeople into the kingdom. Ironically, the woman with the sordid past became an evangelist and brought many people to Christ.

In addition to the Samaritan woman, Luke 8 tells us about Mary Magdalene, Joanna, and Susanna, who became a part of Jesus' support team. Jesus is no different today. He wants women to be a part of His current support team. We needn't think of society or the church as paternalistic. This is God's church and His kingdom, and He wants women just like you involved in ministry with Him.

Compassion is another important lesson Jesus taught us. He often broke with tradition and had little regard for the status quo. One of the greatest examples of this can be found in

Luke 7:11–15, when Jesus stopped a funeral procession and spoke to the woman who had just lost her only son. For a Jewish widow to lose a son was devastating because now she had lost her total support. Her husband and son were both gone. But Jesus had such compassion for this grieving woman that He stopped the funeral procession and touched the dead boy. This was unheard of in Jewish custom, because Jews feared contamination from a corpse. But Jesus told the dead boy to rise, and the boy sat up, spoke, and was returnd to his mother. Jesus understands your grief. Maybe you've lost a child, maybe you've had a miscarriage, maybe you have infertility, maybe you have an illness and you've been told you don't have long to live. Whatever the problem, Jesus understands your grief. His arms are open wide, and He wants to touch you with His compassion, His mercy, and His grace.

Jesus also addressed the issue of aging. God understands aging issues, which is clearly revealed in Luke 13:10–13. In this situation Jesus is preaching in the synagogue where a great crowd had gathered. Suddenly in the middle of His message, He sees an elderly woman who's been bent over for eighteen years, probably with osteoporosis. He calls her over and heals her, and she immediately straightens up. God understands the problems of the elderly. He doesn't just abandon them. He still wants to minister to their needs, whether the needs are physical, emotional, or spiritual.

Jesus is the Master Healer. He healed people throughout His three-year ministry. In the case of Jairus's daughter who had already died, Jesus said, "No, she's just asleep; have faith" (my paraphrase). And He took Peter, James, and John with Him and raised this young girl from the dead. Or consider the story of Peter's mother-in-law, found in Luke 4:38–39. She was struggling with a high fever, but when Jesus touched her, the fever disappeared. Amazingly, when Peter's mother-in-law was miraculously healed, she got out of bed and prepared Jesus and the disciples a meal. I call that being healed to serve.

My mother battled with metastatic colon cancer. Naturally, we prayed for her, and I truly believe she experienced healing because she lived longer than anyone with that type of cancer in this area. She was able to live almost five years after her original diagnosis, and during that time she continued to serve in her women's circle, in her church, and by taking care of her family. When you or your loved one has experienced healing, God does it for a reason and He expects you to continue to serve Him.

CARING FOR WOMEN

How do women want to be treated? How do women deserve to be treated? You deserve to be treated with respect. You deserve to be treated in a loving manner. You deserve forgiveness. You deserve to be communicated with. God desires for you to join with others in ministry opportunities. You also want to be treated with compassion and to be allowed to experience healing. Men are called to minister to their wives, to their girlfriends, and to their relatives in all of the ways we have just discussed. Jesus' example sets the course for all men with respect to caring for women. This is how men are to treat women.

Jesus loves you and He cares for you and He wants to relate to you on a one-to-one basis.

First Peter 5:6-7 says, "Humble yourselves, therefore,

under God's mighty hand, that he may lift you up in due time. Cast all your anxiety on him because he cares for you." That's God's promise to you because He cares for you. In Romans 1:6 we read, "God loves you dearly and has called you to be His very own" (my paraphrase). Jesus loves you and He cares for you and He wants to relate to you on a one-to-one basis. He has your best interest at heart for eternal reasons. There is no greater type of intimacy for a woman than her spiritual pilgrimage with Christ and the relationship that develops between them. Know this: God is not out to get you. God wants to love you through the person of Jesus Christ and through the power of the Holy Spirit. Jesus' love has no limitations, and He will fulfill your needs like no other person could do. I want to encourage you to believe that Jesus really cares for you. No human relationship can satisfy the deep soul-need you have. A relationship with a man cannot match it, no matter how hard you try. No husband can meet that kind of need for his wife; only Jesus can do that. And that's the way He wants it.

ABOUT THE AUTHOR

David Hager, M.D., is the coauthor of *Women at Risk*. He is a medical doctor, specializing in obstetrics and gynecology at Women's Care Center in Lexington, Kentucky. David is on the staff at the University of Kentucky Medical School, serves on the Focus on the Family Physicians Resource Council, and was named one of the top U.S. physicians for women by *Good Housekeeping* and *Ladies Home Journal* magazines. He holds a B.A. degree from Asbury College, an M.D. from the University of Kentucky, and worked at the Centers for Disease Control and Prevention in Atlanta. He was recently named by the Bush Administration to the Advisory Committee for Reproductive Health Drugs in Women at the Food and Drug Administration.

VERSES THAT INSPIRE

When we were still powerless, Christ died for the ungodly. Very rarely will anyone die for a righteous man. . . . But God demonstrates his own love for us in this: While we were still sinners, Christ died for us. (Romans 5:6–8)

This is what the LORD says . . . "Fear not, for I have redeemed you; I have summoned you by name; you are mine." (Isaiah 43:1)

I, the LORD, have called you in righteousness; I will take hold of your hand. (Isaiah 42:6)

For God so loved the world that he gave his one and only Son, that whoever believes in him shall not perish but have eternal life. (John 3:16)

I pray that you, being rooted and established in love, may have power, together with all the saints, to grasp how wide and long and high and deep is the love of Christ. (Ephesians 3:17–18)

The Lord is not slow in keeping his promise, as some understand slowness. He is patient with you, not wanting anyone to perish, but everyone to come to repentance. (2 Peter 3:9)

Living in the Spirit of Unity

❧

THELMA WELLS

*May the God who gives endurance and encouragement give
you a spirit of unity among yourselves.*

—ROMANS 15:5

Have you ever stood in front of the mirror brushing your
hair or brushing your teeth and an idea suddenly popped
into your mind? That's what happened to me not too long
ago. It was at the beginning of last year during my usual rit-
ual of checking in with the Lord and asking Him what He
wants me to focus on during the coming year. I was just

standing there, minding my own business, when suddenly the Lord impressed one word on my spirit: *unity.*

"Unity, Lord? What about unity?" I asked. "I know unity means oneness, with one heart. But, Lord, what are You talking about? Unity in individuals? Unity in families? Unity in the church?"

As He does sometimes, He didn't say a word just then. But I got so mesmerized with the idea of unity that I started studying it from the Word of God. And finally I found His answer. You know what He wants us to do—He wants us to find unity within the body of Christ. But through all my studying and searching of Scripture, I discovered that unity in the body of Christ cannot be had until we have unity with ourselves and unity in our families.

In the midst of all my searching and studying I heard Archbishop Veron Ashe say something that I later realized might have been exactly what God wanted me to do in the area of unity. The archbishop's statement is pretty graphic: "When we meet people flesh to flesh we meet people mess to mess."

As soon as I heard those words out of his mouth, I

thought, *He has a point there.* Now stick with me as I find my way to the point.

For over twenty years I've been teaching cultural diversity to corporations, telling them what happens in the first six to eight seconds when we meet people. You know what happens, don't you? Within the first six to eight seconds of meeting somebody, we decide if we're going to let that person into our life or not. Be honest, you know you do. You look at what they have on. If they don't have on the right cashmere coat or the right shade of lipstick or maybe their hair isn't the way you think it should be—immediately, if not sooner, we decide whether or not we're going to let them become a part of our lives. We even quickly evaluate things like eye contact, facial expression, how we shake hands with each other, or their position in life. I know we do it, because I've done it myself.

Let me tell you a story about me that I am *not* proud of—because from this experience that happened to me about ten years ago, I discovered something about unity in myself.

One day I was walking out of an office building in downtown Dallas with my business suit on. (I was a banker at that time.) I walked out of this big, fancy high rise and saw a lady walking toward me who wasn't dressed very well. She was worn, torn, and a little dirty. This woman said to me, "Ma'am, would you give me a quarter?" And I did something that I never do. I turned to that woman and said crisply, "No, I don't have a quarter." And I looked at her with disgust. As soon as I did that the Holy Spirit nudged me and made me turn around and say to the lady, "Excuse me, ma'am." She was already walking down the street. "Why do you need a quarter?"

She turned around and quietly said, "I need to get the bus."

"I'm sorry I lied to you," I told her. And I put my hand in my corporate suit pocket and gave the lady all the change I had.

With tears in my eyes, watching her walk across the street, I crossed the street in the other direction, sat in my car, and said, "Thelma, what is wrong with you? Why did you disrespect that woman? Even if you didn't want to give her a quarter, you didn't have to be ugly! You didn't have to speak down to her. You didn't have to treat her like she was nothing!"

That was truly an eye-opening experience for me, because up until then I thought I was so wonderful and sweet and such a good Christian. So how did that happen? It showed me what was really inside me. That way of acting toward that woman—that ugliness—couldn't have come *out* of me unless it was already *in* me. That made me realize something and helped me to understand that voice inside me that bluntly said, "Thelma, I don't care how good you think you are, you have some biases, some prejudices, some preconditioning that you have got to shed!"

Ever since that day I've been working on correcting those biases, removing the prejudices, and undoing that preconditioning, and it's taken me many, many years to make progress. Oh, I've slipped up sometimes, but that experience is indelibly imprinted on my mind. I've finally come up with a method that helps me stay on track. When I see people now, I try not to see them "flesh to flesh," because then I see them "mess to mess." Instead, I try to look at them in their spirit. I try to see them "spirit to spirit."

It's no easy task to look beyond the flesh, to look beyond the mess on the surface and find out what that person's spirit is like. I know full well that I can't do it alone. I can't just say, "Thelma, you're going to do this," and expect it all to be different. No, I need help. I need three things to help me: love, the Spirit, and God. Those three will help you and me find oneness in the body of Christ.

LOVE ONE ANOTHER

The first scripture I want to give you is in the Gospel of John. (I love John. John gets right to the point.) John 13:34–35 says, "A new command I give you: Love one another. As I have loved you, so you must love one another. By this all men will know that you are my disciples, if you love one another."

Notice how many times the phrase "love one another" occurs in those verses. Jesus says, "*Love one another.*" That's once. Then He says, "As I have loved you, . . . *love one another.*" That's twice. And then He ends with, "You are my disciples, if you *love one another.*" That's three times. It's like He's saying, "Love one time for the Father, love two times for the Son, love three times for the Holy Spirit." That's where unity is—love for one another. Unity in the body of Christ, unity in your own spirit, and unity in your home can only be experienced through the perfect, indescribable, unconditional love of God.

I think many of us don't love each other because we don't know how to love ourselves. A lot of women I talk to within the course of a year—either in person or through e-mail—have issues with loving themselves. They admit to me that they feel unworthy of being loved. They tell me they've done something in their past that they feel is so bad, they figure, *How in the world can God forgive me and love me when I've so messed up?* Many of them have even been told that they are not worthy of love, that they're ugly, that they can't do anything right. So many peripherals, if you will, make people feel, *I am not worthy. I can't be loved.* But they are so wrong. There is no one not worthy of God's love. Everyone can be and is loved by God.

> *Unity in the body of Christ, unity in your own spirit, and unity in your home can only be experienced through the perfect, indescribable, unconditional love of God.*

Dwight Thompson said, "You cannot do any more or any less to make God love you any more or any less." That just grabs me. And guess what? God doesn't love me any more than He loves you. He doesn't have any favorites. Knowing that makes me so happy I can't stand it! So the first thing we need to do in order to have unity, to have oneness, one heart—is to understand *who* we are in Christ.

Who are you? That is the question you want to ask yourself right now: *Who am I?* Well, you are more spirit than you are flesh. Do you know that before the foundation of the world you were already on God's mind? I can just imagine in the heavenlies, God having this mammoth warehouse with spirits in it: your spirit, my spirit, everybody's spirit. Before the foundation of the world, before the stars were in space, before the moon was in place, before grass was green, before cows were brown and producing white milk, before that, you were on God's mind. And He said on your birthday He was going to send you down from heaven and block out a portion of time for you to live on earth and then give you the opportunity to go back and live with Him when you decide that He is Jesus Christ.

Psalm 139:13–16 tells us that we are more spirit than we are flesh.

> For you created my inmost being;
>> you knit me together in my mother's womb.
> I praise you because I am fearfully and wonderfully made;
>> your works are wonderful,
>> I know that full well.
> My frame was not hidden from you
>> when I was made in the secret place.
> When I was woven together in the depths of the earth,
>> your eyes saw my unformed body.
> All the days ordained for me
>> were written in your book
>> before one of them came to be.

Now let me describe for you what I believe this scripture is saying. I have three wonderful children, five magnificent grandchildren, and before the world began God knew that those three kids and five grandkids would come to me. Let me tell you what He did. When a woman gets pregnant,

God allows the seed of the woman to be fertilized. As soon as that happens, God's spirit has been placed in that woman. For nine months God, with His majestic knitting needles and with His spirit, knits together organs, systems, blood, skin, eyes, nose, ears, and hands. He weaves it all perfectly together and puts in everything we need for doing what He wants us to do on this earth. Through His creation of Adam, He has blown His breath into that spirit, and that spirit becomes a living soul. In nine months it bursts forth crying, and you know it's alive. But that spirit has come from heaven to live on earth, and the predestined plan for the spirit is to go back to its Creator—to go back to Jesus Christ.

Within that flesh—within my flesh, within your flesh— our spirit guards and rules. We allow it sometimes to rule negatively, and we allow it sometimes to rule positively. The negative ruling is the flesh—the sinful nature or the carnal nature that we have. The positive ruling is the spirit of God that every person has in them whether they receive Jesus Christ or not. We all have that spirit. Some people call it a conscience, but I call mine the Holy Spirit since I have received the gift of adoption into the body of Christ. When we meet people "spirit to spirit" then, we know that God has made them. We know that these people were made just like you and I, "fearfully and wonderfully made," knit together by God.

When we know that God is love and that God's love is unconditional, when we know that God made all of us in His image and filled us with His spirit, then we can see someone "spirit to spirit" rather than just "flesh to flesh."

I have a plaque on my wall at home that says, "Love is acceptance without condition." When we see people, we can accept those people and love those people. Now we don't necessarily have to love or even like what they do—I know several people who I love but I don't *like* what they do. But I look through them and see that God has made each of them a precious person. Then I know I've got to love them into the kingdom of God. That's what unity in the church means, that's what unity in the home means, that's what unity in your own personal self means—having love in you as God loves.

But loving people as God loves them without condition is *not* easy. You know why that isn't easy? Because we have all these other "influence-ees" and "influence-ers" out there who tell us how to think about people. That's what really happened to me when I met that lady on the street so many years ago. Somewhere, somehow I had been conditioned how to think about this woman: *Get a job, go bathe, and what is your major malfunction?* I think all that went through my head when I saw that woman. Unfortunately I was seeing her "flesh to flesh," not "spirit to spirit."

So what can we do that's concrete; what can we put our hands on that will bring real unity to the body of Christ? There are several things.

A NEW YOU

The first thing we ought to do is to experience the new birth in Christ. Romans 10:9 has a simple plan of salvation: "If you confess with your mouth, 'Jesus is Lord' and believe in your heart that God raised him from the dead, you will be saved."

That is so cut-and-dried, so simple, that a lot of people miss it. I have heard people say to me, "I've got to get my life together before I can come to Jesus." And I tell them, "You can't get your life together by yourself; you're not that cute or that smart." It just won't happen.

Some say, "I'm just not ready because I want to party and have a good time. If I give my life to Christ, I won't have a good time." I want to tell you that the best times and the best parties I've been to have been Holy Ghost parties—parties with church people. And the best times I've had have been my own intimate times with Jesus. There is none like Him. Nothing else will do. Jesus is really my magnificent obsession. And He can be yours too. That's really what He wants.

Second Corinthians 5:17–19 says, "Therefore, if anyone is in Christ, he is a new creation; the old has gone, the new has come! All this is from God, who reconciled us to himself through Christ and gave us the ministry of reconciliation: that God was reconciling the world to himself in Christ, not counting men's sins against them."

Isn't that wonderful? If we accept Jesus Christ, we become a new creation. Just as I mentioned earlier, He said in effect, "Not only do you become a new creation, but you are then able to accept a new commandment: to love one another." So the first thing we need to do is to experience a new birth in Jesus Christ. Once we do that, our heart and our mind are open to doing the next thing: We need to have union with Christ and dwell as brothers and sisters.

UNITY WITH CHRIST AND OTHERS

Psalm 133:1–3 says,

> How good and pleasant it is
> > when brothers live together in unity!
> It is like precious oil poured on the head,
> > running down on the beard,
> running down on Aaron's beard,
> > down upon the color of his robes.
> It is as if the dew of Hermon
> > were falling on Mount Zion.
> For there the LORD bestows his blessing,
> > even life forevermore.

The first verse of this is so poignant. It says, How good, how pleasant it is for you and me, for men and women, boys and girls, to dwell in unity, one with the other. You know what happens when we dwell in unity with one another—we're able to have relationships that are powerful and meaningful.

I've been married to my husband for over forty years. For the first fifteen years of our marriage, I tried to change him. I wanted to make him

> *When we dwell in unity with one another we're able to have relationships that are powerful and meaningful.*

in my image. When we were courting for six years, he was just fine, but the week after I married him, I saw some stuff I didn't like. I guess it was there all the time, but love is blind. And after "the toothpaste incident"—you know what I mean —I started looking at him funny. So I tried to change this man into my image for fifteen years. He kept telling me, "What you see is what you get. You married me. This is the way I am, and this is the way I'm going to be."

But I was thinking, *You think so, huh? I'm going to do my best to change you.* Well, sometimes I'm slow. It took me fifteen years to realize I couldn't change that man. And the reason I tried to change him was that I didn't feel good about me. That's the way it is when you have some issues—you try to transfer those issues to somebody else. When I got married, I was very young and in college. I had not planned to have children soon, but seven months after we got married I got pregnant with our first child. My life just was *not* going the way it should have been, and it was all his fault! You know it takes two, but it was all *his* fault.

So there I was in school, trying to buy a house, having a new baby, and with a husband starting a new business. And when that baby was only seven months old I got pregnant *again*. (I'm stopping right here to say, Don't do that!) So there I was, trying to graduate from college, and I was blaming my husband: "If it hadn't been for you, if you didn't act like this . . ." And finally I got so depressed that I started imagining all kinds of things; I started thinking I was falling out. The doctor said, "No, Thelma, you're not falling out. If you faint, you don't know what's going on around you. What you're doing is having a major pity party. You need to get on the good foot."

During my quiet time, I started thinking about myself and thinking about the wonderful support and people I had around me, and I started wondering, *Why am I feeling so irritable with this man? Actually he hasn't done anything to me to make me upset.* So I started studying my Bible and thinking about what was going on. And it dawned on me: "Thelma, have you ever read 1 Corinthians 13?"

"Oh, my goodness, in fact I had it read in my wedding ceremony. What is so special about that?"

"Go back and read it."

And so I did. You know 1 Corinthians 13—it's the chapter on love that starts out, "If I speak in the tongues of men and of angels, but have not love. . . ." Well, let me summarize, or better yet, paraphrase it for you. This chapter says there is a bond deep within that binds us one to another. It's the glue of authentic love that expresses itself in compassion and concern, in caring for each other—in coming to the aid of each other personally with no strings attached.

When I read that complete chapter for myself I thought, *Thelma Wells, who are you? Who are you in relation to your husband?* So I turned in my Bible to 1 Corinthians 7 and read that chapter where Paul talks about marriage. Then I said,

"Holy Spirit, help me to get in touch with me, to get in oneness with me, to become one in unity with me so I can be the kind of wife that You are calling for in the last days. A wife who will love and support her husband, a wife who will make him feel good about what he's doing, who will help him know that his position in his home is not threatened." I started doing that and worked hard at rebuilding a relationship with my husband that could have been destroyed because of my own insecurities. God has just done marvelous things in our marriage.

Many years have passed since those first fifteen years, and they've been wonderful years of friendship, of oneness. And I've discovered that in the oneness God has planted in me there is oneness in my family, which means that we can pray together. There isn't any problem that we can't pray about together, and there certainly have been many problems in our lives. We've had financial situations, we've had children rebelling, we've had business failures, we've had health issues. Many, many things have come up. But because of that unity between my husband and myself, we know now that we can stand in any situation, not always agreeing, but always agreeing to disagree and remain agreeable.

It's a fact that my husband and I have not had an argument in over twenty years. It is also a fact that we could have. But we have always agreed that if one of us found ourself getting a little hot under the collar, we would call a time-out. We'd go into a different room, and later we'd come back and talk to each other with respect, with oneness. We also agreed never go to sleep angry at each other. We have never gone to sleep angry at each other in the last twenty years, although, to be quite honest, we have had a few sleepless nights. But in the middle of the night, one of us will say, "Okay, let's talk"; and we're able to talk through anything.

That oneness between husband and wife, that oneness in our family, carries over into the body of Christ. If I can have that unity at home, then I can also carry it over to my church, to my community, to my leisure, to my business, to everything. I can love you in spite of you, according to the *agape* love that is shed abroad in my heart. Wow, that's really unity.

Unity of the Spirit

Now let me give you something else. We need to understand the unity of the Spirit. Ephesians 4:4–5 says, "There is one body and one Spirit—just as you were called to one hope when you were called—one Lord, one faith, one baptism; one God and Father of all, who is over all and through all and in all."

How wonderful that all of us—red and yellow, short, tall, thin, fat, blue eyes, brown eyes, red hair, no hair—have one God. That is amazing! That is called unity in the body. First Corinthians 12:7–11 says:

> Now to each one the manifestation of the Spirit is given for the common good. To one there is given through the Spirit the message of wisdom, to another the message of knowledge by means of the same Spirit, to another faith by the same Spirit, to another gifts of healing by that one Spirit, to another miraculous powers, to another prophecy, to another distinguishing between spirits, to another speaking

in different kinds of tongues, and to still another the interpretation of tongues. All these are the work of one and the same Spirit, and he gives them to each one, just as he determines.

That says to me that there is an abundance of talent, skill, ability, knowledge, and special gifts given to each one of us. But it's all given by one Spirit, and when we take all of those gifts and we measure them together and let them work together as a beautiful tapestry woven together to make a quilt that covers all of us—that's unity.

When we blend all those special abilities together in Christ, the Creator of unity, we get something very special.

First Corinthians 12:26–28 says, "If one part suffers, every part suffers with it; if one part is honored, every part rejoices with it. Now you are the body of Christ, and each one of you is a part of it. And in the church God has appointed first of all apostles, second prophets, third teachers, then workers of miracles, also those having gifts of healing, those able to help others, those with gifts of administration, and those speaking in different kinds of tongues." When we blend all those special gifts, all those special abilities together in Christ, the Creator of unity, we get something very special.

I sing sometimes, but I *cannot* play the piano. I tried. I took lessons for four and a half years! But there was no unity between the black and white keys on the piano and the black and white notes on the page of music. I have no skill, no ability, no aptitude. But I wanted to play the piano like one of my friends, Dr. Shirley Harris. She can play Bach, Beethoven, rock-'n'-roll, gospel, or whatever; but I can't play a thing— it's just all noise. I thought for the first year that either I was making that horrible noise or it was a bad piano that was making that noise come out. So I went out and bought a new piano to help me sound better. But let me tell you—it didn't work. I still couldn't play. But for three years when I was taking piano lessons with no progress, I didn't like Shirley Harris. I told her that too.

I said, "Shirley, I don't like you."

"Why not?" she said.

And I told her. "I can guarantee you, you can play the

piano, but you can't sing. I can sing. But why can't I play the piano?"

Finally one day, as I was trying to coordinate my right hand with my left hand and those notes, a light bulb came on and something in my head said, *Thelma, ask Shirley to play for you when you sing.* What a sensational idea! I had wasted all this time trying to be Shirley when I could have just asked her to play for me. So I went to the telephone, picked it up, and called Shirley.

"Hey, Shirley," I said, "I have a question for you. When I'm invited to sing, would you come and play for me as my pianist?"

In a flash she replied, "Yes, girl, I will. I was waiting for you to ask me to do that."

And guess what happened? She was on the piano, tickling those keys, I was singing, and we were a dynamic duo. That was unity! That was oneness. Her talent was matched with my talent, and we were able to go out and do that. That's what God wants us to do with the body of Christ. Rather than expending energy on something we have no control over, rather than disliking somebody because he or she can do something that we can't do, He wants us to unite our talents as one. He wants us to look at each individual, to see the spirit of this individual, and to match up with the spirit, the talent, the gifts of this individual to create a wonderful, beautiful, king-size tapestry as if God took His knitting needles and wove us together. God tells us, "I need you to weave together the people, the plan, the resources, and everything I've given you, so you can be everything I've called you to be—living in oneness with your family, oneness with your church." We can do that, but it takes a change of mind.

YOU CAN B-E-E THE BEST

I wear a bumblebee pin everywhere I go. I've worn it now for the last twenty-some years. People always ask me, "Thelma, why do you wear a bumblebee?" Well, aerodynamically speaking, the bumblebee is not supposed to be able to fly. Its body is too big; its wingspan is too shallow. It shouldn't fly, but it does. It does exactly what God intended for it to do.

Prior to my knowledge of this information about the bee, I had asked God to give me something that I could leave with people to help them remember what I said, long after they had forgotten my name and my face—because none of this is about me; it's all about Him. Well, one day as I was entering my church building, wearing a bee on my lapel, a woman said to me, "Thelma Wells, that sure is a pretty bee, and every time you wear that bee, remember, 'You can be the best of what you want to be.'"

Just as soon as she finished saying that, I said under my breath, "Thank You, Lord; that's the perfect thing for me to use." Eventually I coined the phrase, "You can B-E-E the best."

Be aware of who you are.

Eliminate the negatives from your mind.

Expect the best from yourself and other people.

That equals success.

Booker T. Washington said, "Success is not to be measured so much by the status one has attained in life but rather by the obstacles one has overcome while trying to succeed." Anytime there is unity, there will be obstacles to overcome. But God has given us everything it takes to overcome the obstacles of looking at people's flesh and seeing what we think we see. He will help us look at people's spirits and understand that He made them, that they're special in His sight. Then we can help them become even better by giving a smile, a tender touch, a nice hello, and accepting them just as they are.

Through love and the Spirit and with God's help, we can live with one heart. We can create unity wherever we go—in ourselves, in our families, and in the church.

ABOUT THE AUTHOR

Thelma Wells is the founder and president of A Woman of God Ministries, L.L.C. As a highly acclaimed national and international motivational speaker, she is a key speaker with the Women of Faith tour. Thelma is also a media personality and professor at Master's Divinity School and Master's Graduate School of Divinity. She is founder of the Mother of Zion Leadership Mentoring Program as well.

VERSE THAT INSPIRE

You are all sons of God through faith in Christ
Jesus. . . . There is neither Jew nor Greek, slave nor
free, male nor female, for you are all one in Christ
Jesus. (Galatians 3:26, 28)

If you have any encouragement from being united
with Christ, if any comfort from his love, if any
fellowship with the Spirit, if any tenderness and
compassion, then make my joy complete by being
like-minded, having the same love, being one in
spirit and purpose. (Philippians 2:1–2)

Finally, all of you, live in harmony with one
another; be sympathetic, love as brothers, be compassionate and humble. (1 Peter 3:8)

May the God who gives endurance and encouragement give you a spirit of unity among yourselves as you follow Christ Jesus, so that with one heart and mouth you may glorify the God and Father of our Lord Jesus Christ. (Romans 15:5–6)

Does God Deserve Our Trust?

BEVERLY LaHAYE AND
LORI LaHAYE SCHECK

The LORD is good, a refuge in times of trouble.
He cares for those who trust in him.

—NAHUM 1:7

How big is God in your life? Sometimes He is very small when we want to take charge of our own affairs. Only when we get into trouble or difficulty do we want God to step forward and work things out for us. We want God around when we pray for His help in times of trouble, but when things are running smoothly we move ahead and fail to ask for His guidance and wisdom.

We create the size of our God by putting Him in a box of our own making and limiting His desire to be all that He wants to be in our lives. His ways are not always our ways! Have you ever asked God to heal someone and when He didn't you became upset with Him? Have you ever asked God to work out a circumstance and He didn't do it the way you wanted it done, so you felt God had abandoned you?

(*Lori*) When God brought our family to Alabama, my daughter was going to be a junior in high school and my oldest son was going into the eighth grade. Needless to say, they were not too happy about being taken from their home and their friends and starting out in a new place where they knew no one. I prayed that God would take care of my kids and help them develop friendships quickly in our new state. I believed playing on a school sports team would help that. As soon as we arrived in our new home, I set about to sign them up to play sports for the school. Imagine my dismay when I learned that the home we purchased was not in the same county as the Christian school the kids would be attending, which by Alabama state regulations rendered my children ineligible to play sports for a full year. I lobbied the state athletic association in letters and phone calls. I even drove down to the state capital to attend an association committee meeting to plead my children's case in person. Unfortunately they were not sympathetic to our plight and would not make an exception. I was devastated. I had prayed. I had asked my friends and family to pray. I felt God hadn't listened or didn't appreciate the situation my children were in. I was so disappointed that God hadn't answered my prayers. I had limited God and put Him in a box. I had prayed that God would take care of my situation, and then I told Him how He should handle it.

A God-box is created when we have an overinflated view of who we are and an underinflated view of who God is. It is created when we do not adequately trust God to be God and to work out His will in His way and in His time. Complete trust is a difficult thing. It requires us to *let go!* That often overused phrase, *Let go and let God*, is all about trust. I know most of us would say that we do trust God. I believe we all want to trust God. Oftentimes, however, that's when our God-box comes into play. We trust God as long as the outcome is what we want it to be. I believe that our ability to trust God completely is dependent on our view of who God is.

Trust does not come naturally to most of us. It is true that some temperaments have greater difficulty than others in learning to put their absolute trust in Almighty God. God often deals with us differently as individuals because we each have our own combination of temperaments.

(Beverly) My daughter, Lori (who represents the younger generation), and I have discussed some of the hard lessons that God puts before us to help us learn how to trust Him more. The very capable Choleric woman, who always has things under her control, may feel that she can handle each situation by herself and she does not need to depend on God. It is true that she is very capable, but there are certain times and situations in life that even she cannot work out. She desperately needs to let go of her own control and experience the Holy Spirit's control for her life.

The fun-loving Sanguine woman usually does not take time to even think about her problems and struggles because she has the tendency just to sweep negative things under the rug. She needs to face the realities of life and learn to put her trust in God for all things.

The Melancholy woman, who is often so deep in thought and introspection, needs to put away her negative thinking and learn to live life with a more positive attitude as she puts her trust in God.

Finally, the Phlegmatic woman is often limited by the spirit of fear and anxiety and does not understand that God wants to free her from that bondage and give her power, love, and a sound mind as she trusts Him more.

God, who is the Potter, knows just how to mold our simple clumps of human clay and make us into what He wants us to be. But we have to put our trust in Him and allow Him to mold and make us according to His will.

But indeed, O man, who are you to reply against God? Will the thing formed say to him who formed it, "Why have you made me like this?" Does not the potter have power over the clay, from the same lump to make one vessel for honor and another for dishonor? (Romans 9:20–21 NKJV)

But now, O LORD, You are our Father; we are the clay, and You our Potter; and all we are the work of Your hand. (Isaiah 64:8 NKJV)

One of the oldest hymns we remember says, "Have Thine own way, Lord, have Thine own way; Thou art the potter, I am the clay. Mold me and make me after Thy will, while I am waiting yielded and still."

That is the secret—to be yielded to God so He can mold us. He who created us knows just how He wants to mold us and make us effective for His glory, but we have to put our complete trust in Him and allow Him to change us.

One thing we need to remember is that trusting God does not absolve us of our own responsibility and common sense. There's an old saying that says something like, "Definitely pray, but keep on rowing." In our involvement with Concerned Women for America we strongly advocate praying for our country and our elected officials. We encourage our members to pray specifically about bills coming up for a vote or for various judicial appointments. CWA was founded on the principle of prayer. We also encourage our members to act. We teach people how to write letters to their congressmen. We provide opportunities for people to call their senators or sign petitions on specific issues. The combination of prayer *and* action is essential. In the end, however, the final outcome is up to God. When we have done all that we can, we trust God to accomplish the rest.

It is safe to say that our ability to trust demands a high level of confidence in the person whom we are trusting. As young people we quickly learned with whom we could share our secrets. Every junior higher knows that if you want something broadcast to the entire school, then you tell a certain person. If you want to share something private and have it stay private, then you tell another person. I'm sure many of us can remember painful experiences of how we figured out which person was which. We want to find someone we can trust. That's true in every area of life. We look for the most competent doctors, the most reliable bankers, the most trustworthy pastors. The question that begs to be asked then is, How high is your confidence level in God?

In the other walks of life we have options. If we don't like the way our doctor is treating our illness, then we find another doctor. If we don't believe that our bank is responsible in the way it handles our account, we move our money to another bank. How many people have changed churches because they didn't like the way the pastor did things, or sadly enough, because their pastor demonstrated that he was not worthy of their trust? The point is that in these other areas we have options. When it comes to God, we do not. You definitely don't want to fire God. To trust God, however, has a greater cost factor. You are not just putting your health or your finances into His hands. You are placing your entire future there. That's the time when we have to ask a really hard question . . . hard, that is, if you answer honestly: Does God deserve our trust? There are many ways we can answer this question.

THE INTELLECTUAL ANSWER—OF COURSE!

All you have to do is spend a little time in Scripture and you can see time and time again that God proved Himself faithful to His people. Look at the favorite stories from the Old Testament: David and Goliath, Moses and the Red Sea,

Daniel in the lion's den, the three men and the fiery furnace. Look at the life of Christ, how He touched people and healed them, how He taught them and forgave them. They are all lessons in God's faithfulness and trustworthiness.

In addition to biblical examples of God's faithfulness, the Scriptures hold many admonitions from God to trust in Him.

Cast all your anxiety on him because he cares for you. (1 Peter 5:7)

The LORD is good, a refuge in times of trouble. He cares for those who trust in him. (Nahum 1:7)

In you our fathers put their trust; they trusted and you delivered them. They cried to you and were saved; in you they trusted and were not disappointed. (Psalm 22:4–5)

Trust in the LORD forever, for the LORD, the LORD, is the Rock eternal. (Isaiah 26:4)

If for no other reason, we should choose to trust God because He has told us to. The problem is that oftentimes doing what we have been told to do, in times of emotional stress, is very difficult. The truth is, however, most of us don't always function at this "intellectual" level.

There are other answers to the question, Does God deserve our trust?

THE EMOTIONAL ANSWER—I HAVE TO!

(*Lori*) When we moved our children to Alabama it was very difficult on the two older ones. Our oldest son, Nathan, was in the eighth grade and was definitely not happy with the decision. He was fourteen, which typically isn't a very pretty age under the best of circumstances. Add to that the emotional trauma of losing all your friends and having to start from scratch in a place you really don't want to be. If that weren't enough (in addition to the sports issue), he had left behind a young lady of whom he was very fond. All in all it was not a good year for him. He hurt so deeply and became so angry. He had always been a very exuberant child demonstrating a zest for life that was contagious. He had an impish way of making everything into a competition, and he was going to be the one on top! After our move, I watched my energetic, enthusiastic son become apathetic and sullen. His grades dropped, and he became detached and very emotional. It broke my heart.

When the inevitable happened—the girl back home broke up with him—I thought I was going to lose him completely. I cried out to God because there was nothing I could do to fix it. Every circumstance was out of my control, and I had to place him completely in God's hands or lose my mind with worry. I continually reminded myself that God loved this boy much more than I ever could and He was big enough to take care of my son. And take care of him He did! God has brought him so far. Three years after our move Nathan is his exuberant self again and a member of the National Honor Society and the president of the junior class. He has made many good friendships here, and his relationship to Christ is much more real and personal than it was before.

Sometimes life just gets too big for us to handle. Those are the times when we find ourselves on our faces crying out to God. We have to put our trust in God because it is absolutely the only thing we can do. If you have a sick child or a loved one who is dying, if someone you care about has strayed away from God, you know what I'm talking about. There is not one thing you can do to change the situation, and the only way you can get out of bed and function each morning is to know that God is there and that He cares. I know for most women (and a lot of men) our natural inclination is to worry and fret. When we were going through that hard time with our son, I had to daily remind myself that Nathan was in God's hands. God would take care of him. He had to, because I knew I sure couldn't.

THE TYPICAL ANSWER—NOT YET!

(Beverly) The reality is that we often don't want to trust God until we've tried to fix the problem ourselves first. Also, we think we might not like the way God fixes it. I don't believe this is always a conscious decision on our part. Many of us set about to deal with a situation and we don't intentionally leave God out; we just forget to include Him. Sometimes I think we

don't really comprehend how much God wants to be involved in our everyday lives. We go along day to day and we just function: take care of our families, go to work, make decisions, minister at church. We really don't give God a second thought until something big comes up. Oftentimes we tend to react first, think second, act third, and pray as a last resort.

I think we would all agree that of course God does deserve our trust. If someone were to come up and ask, "Do you trust God?" most of us would say that we do. What does it mean, then, when we look at our lives and realize that we really haven't trusted God in our day-to-day world? What does it mean when it takes something catastrophic to make us turn our lives over to Him? This is where it is important to step back and evaluate our view of God.

Certainly it is a universally held position that God is big. Anyone who has any belief in God at all perceives Him to be the Almighty God of the universe. Those of us who believe the Bible know that He is the one who created all things. He created the miracles of seasons and the universe, of life and birth and death. The Bible is full of examples of His greatness: parting the Red Sea, making time stand still, repeatedly protecting His people from their enemies. He provided manna in the desert for His people, He helped Gideon's small army defeat the Midianites, and He sent the plagues of Egypt. He does big things in a big way. We trust God for the big things in our lives. We trust Him for salvation. We trust Him to sustain our lives.

Unfortunately, when we get too much beyond that, we have a bit of trouble with our trust level. When it comes to trusting God to provide for our needs, to take care of our children, to provide us with a spouse—to be involved in the circumstances of our lives—that's when we run into trouble. Somehow we prefer to worry and scheme about things in our everyday world, but we are willing to commit the larger issues into God's hands. It is almost as if we think God is too big to be concerned about our little issues. We are more than willing to put our nation's troubles into His hands, but we won't bother Him with whether we should send our kids to camp or where the money will come from. Does God care about our husband's employment? Can we trust God to help work out our marriage difficulties?

God is holy. We all know that. We count on it. We know

God to be holy, righteous, and just, and we also know that He wants us to be like Him—to be holy and righteous and just. We also know that sometimes God allows things to come into our lives to shape us and test our character. Because of that, I believe that sometimes we are a little cautious about trusting God because we're afraid of what He may bring into our lives in order to teach us something or to test us. Just look at the life of Job. It is fairly safe to say that none of us would care to walk in Job's shoes. Many of us are afraid that if we place something in God's hands, He might take it away from us in order to teach us a lesson. Perhaps we may even be afraid that He allows hard things to come into our lives in order to punish us for not being holy and righteous enough.

The truth about God is that He is big, He is sovereign, and He is holy. Instead of driving us away from God, these things should make us run to Him. There is one other aspect of who God is that we all too often overlook when it comes to trusting Him: He loves us so much. Scripture is full of demonstrations of His love and mercy. What's more, God wants good things for our lives. He is not some cruel taskmaster who derives pleasure out of tormenting His little minions. Look at what Scripture says:

"For I know the plans I have for you," declares the LORD, "plans to prosper you and not to harm you, plans to give you hope and a future." (Jeremiah 29:11)

And we know that in all things God works for the good of those who love him, who have been called according to his purpose. (Romans 8:28)

And why do you worry about clothes? See how the lilies of the field grow. They do not labor or spin. Yet I tell you that not even Solomon in all his splendor was dressed like one of these. If that is how God clothes the grass of the field, which is here today and tomorrow is thrown into the fire, will he not much more clothe you, O you of little faith? (Matthew 6:28–30)

God loves us and wants us to have an abundant life. Yes, sometimes He does allow difficult circumstances to come into our lives, but that doesn't change who God is or how much He cares about us. Some of the difficulties we experience are of our own making, yet we still manage to blame God for them.

God has promised so many good things to us. He promised He would never leave us or forsake us. He promised to supply all our needs. God knows when each sparrow falls to the ground and how many hairs we have on our head. That means He really knows about the stuff that hurts us or frightens us. I don't know about you, but I can be quite an expert in the area of worry. Yet God has said in Philippians 4:6 not to be anxious about anything, but instead to place our concerns at His feet. God doesn't want us to be afraid. Second Timothy 1:7 says, "For God has not given us a spirit of fear, but of power and of love and of a sound mind" (NKJV).

Does trusting God mean that everything will work out just the way we want it to and that we'll live happily ever after? No, it doesn't. That's a God-box. Let me ask you something. When you plan or scheme or worry about something, does it turn out the way you want it to and you live happily ever after? I am sure the answer is no.

That may be the whole point: Whether you trust God with your life does not change the fact that you still really have no control over your circumstances. You may think you can affect the outcome of a situation, but more likely than not, you just get in the way. The reality is, none of us has control of our life. We have no guarantee what tomorrow might bring. Then the question is, Why do we spend so much time worrying over things over which we have no control? The true joy of trusting God is the peace He provides when you do. Trusting God to do things in His way and in His time is the only way we can have true and lasting peace, and I guarantee the outcome will be exactly what God has in mind for you.

> "For my thoughts are not your thoughts, neither
> are your ways my ways," declares the LORD. "As
> the heavens are higher than the earth, so are my
> ways higher than your ways and my thoughts than
> your thoughts." (Isaiah 55:8–9)

The answer will come in the exact time frame God has for you. Too often we are in a hurry for God to work things out, but He has His own time schedule. That's still part of trusting.

(Lori) My mother has often had to remind me that God says to be still and know that He is God. Waiting on God is hard. Sometimes it feels like He isn't doing anything. That's another part of the God-box. The truth is that God wants us to wait on Him, and while we are waiting, God is working.

So if our ability to trust God completely is dependent on our view of who God is, then how can we improve our view of God? First of all, it is important to view yourself correctly. This is the hard part because it requires simple honesty. We are flawed creatures. We have a sin nature. Not only are we flawed, but we are limited. We don't know what tomorrow brings. We don't know the "big picture" of our lives or anyone else's. Scripture teaches that we can't add one more day to our lives or one more inch to our height by worry or anything else we might try to do. Think about the things you worry about or fuss over. Can you really do anything at all to make things turn out a certain way? This is a difficult concept because most of us like to feel some semblance of control of our lives. The problem is that we really don't have that control. What we do have is the ability to choose how we will manage our response to life's circumstances: worry, fret, anger, and frustration, or peace, joy, and confidence that only come from trusting God.

Not only is it important to know yourself well, but it is essential to know God well. I love to read the Psalms. I love to read how David talked to God. This is a man who clearly knew who God is and understood both His greatness as well as His goodness. No wonder God regarded David as "a man after God's own heart." Reading God's Word is the best way to know and really understand who God is. Reading is just the start. It is also important to believe what you read and to believe that it relates personally to you. The Bible has often been called God's love letter to us. It's true. He wrote the Bible so we could know Him better and begin to understand how very much He loves us.

It is also important to talk to God frequently. It is hard to trust someone you never talk to. The more you know Him, the more you will love Him and want to put your full trust in Him. God, who has promised to never leave us or forsake us, puts out His loving arms and invites us to come to Him and completely trust Him. You will never be sorry!

ABOUT THE AUTHORS

Beverly LaHaye is the founder and chairman of Concerned Women for America (CWA). She has authored eight books and coauthored seven books, both fiction and nonfiction; one of the best known is *The Act of Marriage,* written with her husband, Tim. Beverly currently serves on the boards of Liberty University, Childcare International, and the International Right to Life Federation.

Lori LaHaye Scheck is a wife and a stay-at-home mom with four children. She holds a degree in communications from Cedarville University and has been very involved for many years in the worship and drama ministries of her church.

VERSES THAT INSPIRE

Why do you worry about clothes? See how the lilies of the field grow. They do not labor or spin. Yet I tell you that not even Solomon in all his splendor was dressed like one of these. If that is how God clothes the grass of the field, which is here today and tomorrow is thrown into the fire, will he not much more clothe you, O you of little faith? (Matthew 6:28–30)

For my thoughts are not your thoughts, neither are your ways my ways," declares the LORD. "As the heavens are higher than the earth, so are my ways higher than your ways and my thoughts than your thoughts." (Isaiah 55:8–9)

The LORD is good, a refuge in times of trouble. He cares for those who trust in him. (Nahum 1:7)

Many are the woes of the wicked,
    but the LORD's unfailing love
    surrounds the man who trusts in him.
Rejoice in the LORD and be glad, you righteous;
    sing, all you who are upright in heart!
    (Psalm 32:10–11)

He who dwells in the shelter of the Most High
    will rest in the shadow of the Almighty.
I will say of the Lord, "He is my refuge and my fortress,
    my God, in whom I trust." (Psalm 91:1–2)

Extraordinary Women (EWomen), a ministry of the American Association of Christian Counselors (AACC), is a faith-based movement focused on taking women closer to the heart of God. For more information on our dynamic training programs, conferences, resources, and membership benefits, visit *Ewomen.net* or call 1-800-526-8673 or write P.O. Box 739, Forest, VA 24551.

AACC is a membership organization of more than 50,0000 clinical, pastoral, and lay counselors dedicated to promoting excellence in faith-based counseling. Post Office Box 739, Forest, VA 24551; 1-800-526-8673; *www.aacc.net*

Shine Magazine is a centerpiece publication for Extraordinary Women. *Shine* bridges the gap between a woman's outer and inner beauty. Each issue celebrates the spiritual, intellectual, and physical aspects of womanhood. Isaiah 60:1 "Arise, SHINE, for your light has come, and the glory of the LORD rises upon you."

YOU ARE AN EXTRAORDINARY WOMAN!

*I*f *A Woman and Her God* gave you a glimpse of the extraordinary life, you'll want to get *Praying through Life's Problems* and *The Joy of Marriage God's Way.*

As you read the chapters of *Praying through Life's Problems* from Stormie Omartian, Joni Eareckson Tada, Leslie Vernick, Catherine Hart Weber, Joseph and Mary Ann Mayo, Linda Mintle, and Diane Langberg, you will come to a fresh perspective of pain, a new encouragement in your struggles, and a greater confidence in approaching God Himself. And out of that will come a faith that not only endures, but that runs deeper than any darkness.

ISBN 1-59145-203-1

Newlyweds to empty nesters can benefit from the wisdom within the pages of *The Joy of Marriage God's Way*—either by getting started on the right foot, or finding there is hope within a broken or stagnant marriage. As you read these chapters from Beverly LaHaye, Julie Clinton, Joyce Penner, Barbara Rosberg, Deb Laaser, Carrie Oliver, and Laurie Hall, you will discover how to establish and maintain the kind of marriage God intended for you to have—one of extraordinary joy!

ISBN 1-59145-202-3

AVAILABLE AT BOOKSTORES EVERYWHERE